ADVENTURES IN CIRCLES

QUILT DESIGNS FROM START TO FINISH

LEIGH E. McDONALD

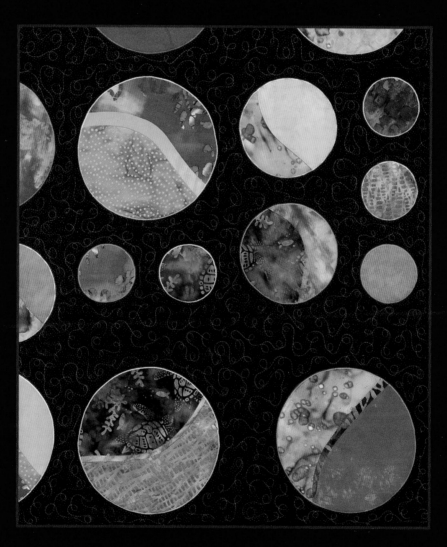

Martingale®
& COMPANY

Adventures in Circles: Quilt Designs from Start to Finish
© 2008 by Leigh E. McDonald

That Patchwork Place® is an imprint of
Martingale & Company®.

Martingale & Company
20205 144th Ave. NE
Woodinville, WA 98072-8478 USA
www.martingale-pub.com

Credits

President & CEO ~ Tom Wierzbicki
Publisher ~ Jane Hamada
Editorial Director ~ Mary V. Green
Managing Editor ~ Tina Cook
Developmental Editor ~ Karen Costello Soltys
Technical Editor ~ Laurie Baker
Copy Editor ~ Melissa Bryan
Design Director ~ Stan Green
Production Manager ~ Regina Girard
Illustrator ~ Laurel Strand
Cover & Text Designer ~ Stan Green
Photographer ~ Brent Kane

Mission Statement

Dedicated to providing quality products and service
to inspire creativity.

Printed in China
13 12 11 10 09 08   8 7 6 5 4 3 2 1

Library of Congress Cataloging-in-Publication Data
Library of Congress Control Number: 2008012226

ISBN: 978-1-56477-802-4

DEDICATION
To my grandmother, Nellie Williamson, who passed away a week after the inspiration for this book was born and never even knew about it. The first quilt I ever received was made by Grandma Nellie. Without her influence, I might never have entered the world of quilting.

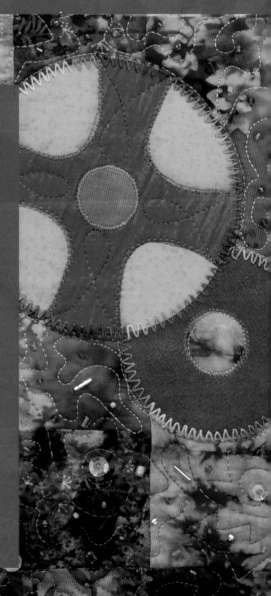

ACKNOWLEDGMENTS
I want to thank:

The Olfa Company for providing me with such wonderful tools;

Family and friends who supported and encouraged me during the writing of this book, especially Linda Cline for quilting "Nellie's Circle Four Patch," Karen Hinkle and Barb Feldmann for their help in proofing the manuscript, Mary Kapenekas for sharing the fabric, and Polly Gilmore for the ideas on ways to use beads;

Carrye Kearns for helping me with the photographs for the publisher;

The Victorian Quilt Shop for allowing me to take photos in their classroom;

Kim Montagnese, Kim Svoboda, and Susan Leslie Lumsden, who graciously shared their artistic endeavors in the "Gallery";

My husband, who took me out to dinner, and cooked and cleaned when I was writing. I couldn't have done it without you, Bill;

And lastly, to editor Karen Soltys, for seeing the potential of the manuscript and helping make it a reality.

CONTENTS

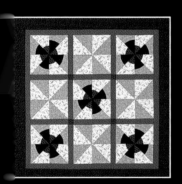

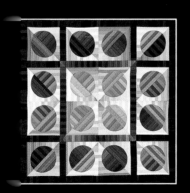

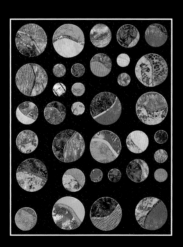

PROJECTS

INTRODUCTION

There are very rare occasions when inspiration strikes me like a flash of lightning, but the brainstorm for this book hit me just that way. One rainy day I was stuffing workshop proposals into envelopes to send out to quilt-show coordinators and quilt shops. I glanced at the cover of one of the proposals and saw a photograph of "Marbelous Marbles" (see page 74), a quilt that featured appliquéd circles. Suddenly I had an idea for another quilt with appliquéd circles, and then another! The storm of ideas came fast and furious—after three days I had sketches for at least six different quilt blocks, and even some complete quilt designs. The catalyst for all these ideas was a tool I had received that week, the Olfa Rotary Circle Cutter, which is a wonderful gadget that makes cutting circles a dream.

After the initial idea took shape, another theme helped guide me throughout the process of designing the quilts and writing this book. My thoughts constantly turned to things that directly and indirectly relate to my family, especially my grandmother Nellie. "Nellie's

Circle Four Patch" (page 31) was named after my grandmother, and I tried to honor her by choosing fabrics that she would have used. The design for the quilt "Clockworks" (page 59) was triggered by a clear acrylic paperweight filled with floating watch parts. This small curio was given to my great uncle, a watch repairman, many years ago, and it is mine now. Like the paperweight, "Clockworks" reminds me of my great uncle every time I see it.

Your quilts, and the stories behind them, will be different from mine, but I hope this book can help you experience your own flash of inspiration. I have written it with both the experienced beginner and the advanced quilter in mind. If you are a beginner, it's best if you already have some experience with rotary cutting and basic piecing techniques, and I suggest you read the book from start to finish to make sure you have the required skills for a successful project. "Basic Quiltmaking Techniques," beginning on page 90, is a how-to reference section on my favorite, specific quiltmaking techniques—the ones that I teach

my beginning students. More advanced quilters will already have their own favorite methods for sewing borders and bindings and may not even need to use this information. Whatever your skill level, watch for the little tip boxes throughout the book. They describe time-saving methods, as well as tricks for using certain tools, that can make a process quicker or simpler.

Before you jump into any of the eight projects, I encourage you to read the sections geared specifically toward making circles. In "Tools" on page 8, I've compiled useful information on some of the new, specialized products for cutting and drawing circles, as well as a general listing of tools and gadgets that I rely on. Check out "Fabrics" on page 11 for ways to change the flavor of a quilt from traditional to contemporary, or vice versa. Specific techniques involved in appliquéing circles are explained in "Working with Circles" on page 16, while "Embellishing Tools, Tips, and Techniques" on page 21 is packed with details on giving your quilts extra flair with special threads, fabrics, and beads.

I have included a mixture of beginner to advanced quilts as well as traditional-style quilts with a contemporary flavor. For additional inspiration and ideas, check out the "Gallery" on page 69. Here you will see variations of some of the quilt projects included in the book, as well as circle quilts created by other quilt artists. Let your imagination soar as you look at these wonderful quilts.

For those of you who love hand appliqué or hand quilting, all the projects in this book can be adapted to hand methods. I prefer machine techniques because of their speediness, but I love to add beads and sequins to my quilts and I do this by hand. Many good books have been written on hand appliqué, and your local library may prove to be a wonderful resource for books on that subject and other quilting topics.

When your quilt top is finished, be sure to read "Quilting Ideas" on page 81 for tips, methods, and designs for quilting your circle quilts.

Whatever your interest, I hope you will find something in these pages that challenges you, whether it is a new tool, a new method for appliqué, or a project that catches your eye. Most of all, I hope you have fun making the quilts in this book. Happy Quilting!

—*Leigh*

Tools

Most of the tools you will use for circle quilts are the same ones you use for other types of quilting. You may already have many of the items listed below. I've also included a few tools specific to circle quilts, as well as some products and gadgets that are fun to use or make a technique easier.

Acrylic rulers. These rulers come in several sizes and are for use with rotary cutters. A 6" x 24" ruler is a good starting size for cutting fabric pieces. You will also need a 12" or 12½" square ruler for squaring up blocks.

Appliqué needles. For sewing beads to fabric, I prefer a size 10 appliqué needle, which is thin enough to accommodate a bead but stronger than a beading needle for pulling through fabric. You can also use these for hand stitching the appliqués to the background, if that is your preference.

Beading threads. Often made of nylon, these threads are made to resist abrasion and slide easily through beads. Some commonly found brands are Nymo and C-Lon. Conso upholstery thread is also very useful for some beading applications.

Clear appliqué foot. Visibility is crucial when appliquéing, and this foot allows you to see in front of the needle as you stitch around the edges of any appliqué.

Compass. This tool can be used to mark circles up to 10" in diameter. Find one that can be tightened with a screw so it will not move when you are using it. It is not fun to have a compass that closes up while you are making a circle.

Decorative threads. Multicolored threads, hand-dyed threads, rayon and polyester threads, and even holographic threads are all wonderful to use with some of the techniques in this book. Look for ideas and examples of places to use decorative thread in "Embellishing Tools, Tips, and Techniques" on page 21.

Freezer paper. You'll need this product to make your templates for freezer-paper appliqué. It can be purchased at your local grocery store in the plastic wrap/food storage section.

Microtex sewing-machine needles. These are very fine, sharp needles that are terrific for piecing. I use size 75/11 or 80/12 for piecing. They also work great when zigzag stitching with monofilament on the edge of an appliqué.

Monofilament. Available in clear and a smoke color, monofilament is a very fine nylon or polyester thread. I use monofilament to do machine appliqué that looks like it has been hand stitched.

Olfa Rotary Circle Cutter. This tool is a compass with a rotary cutter built in. It can cut perfect circles up to 8½" in diameter through one or two layers of fabric.

Paper-backed transfer web. Sold by the yard and in packages, this heat-activated sheet of glue comes in lightweight and heavyweight varieties. You will need the lightweight variety for the projects in this book if you choose to use the fusible-web appliqué method. There are many brands of fusible webs on the market, but I have always had good results with Wonder-Under.

Quarter-inch piecing foot. Sew exact ¼" seams consistently with this specialty presser foot.

Rotary cutters. All the pieces for your projects can be cut out with a rotary cutter. For most pieces, a cutter with a 45 mm blade works well, but to cut circles, an 18 mm or 28 mm blade will give the best results.

Rotary cutting mat. You will need to place a rotary mat under your fabric when cutting with a rotary cutter. Buy the largest mat you can afford or that you can fit on your cutting surface.

Sewer's Aid. This liquid silicone product is applied to thread to reduce static and shredding. The liquid is applied differently based on the tension disks in your machine. Be sure to follow the manufacturer's instructions or check with your sewing-machine dealer if you have questions. In general, for machines with metal tension disks, apply the product to the spool of thread by putting the spout of the bottle against the thread on the spool and running it across the threads twice. Then thread the sewing machine as you normally would. For sewing machines with nylon tension disks, such as Pfaff sewing machines, the silicone must be added to the thread after it goes through the tension disks. An easy way to do this is to cut a tiny piece of moleskin (usually used on human feet and found in your local drug store) and stick it to the needle bar/clamp next to or behind the last thread guide before the needle. Put a small amount of Sewer's Aid on the moleskin. Each treatment of Sewer's Aid lasts approximately two hours. Reapply when you start to have problems, such as skipped stitches or shredded thread.

Silk pins. These are excellent for pinning when sewing curves. I use 1½"-long pins because they are easy to grab. Use pins with the thinnest shaft you can find.

Tear-away stabilizer. Using stabilizer on the underside of an appliqué that will be satin stitched helps prevent buckling of the fabric and stitches. Once the stitching is completed, the stabilizer is torn or cut away. Stabilizers are sold by the yard and in packages and are located with the interfacings at a fabric store.

Teflon pressing sheet. You will need this tool to layer the pieces of a fusible appliqué before attaching it to the background fabric in its final position. Remove the paper backing from the individual appliqué pieces and assemble them right

side up on the Teflon pressing sheet; press to fuse the pieces together. Let the appliqué cool, and then peel the fused unit away from the pressing sheet and place in position for the final, permanent fusing. The pressing sheet also can be used over the fusible appliqué to protect the iron from any exposed fusible product or under the fusible-web pieces to protect the ironing board surface.

Thread Heaven. If you use thread, you'll want this product. Created to condition and protect thread, it reduces tangling, decreases thread drag, and extends the life of your thread. I use it on my beading thread to make it stronger and allow it to slide through fabric more easily, and also when I'm doing any type of hand stitching.

Thread stand. This is a terrific item. It allows you to sew with the large cones of decorative thread that won't fit on a standard sewing-machine spool pin. It also helps with threads that need a vertical spool pin to feed correctly. Place it on the table behind your sewing machine and thread under the cover or directly to the first thread guide on your sewing machine. If you use a lot of decorative threads, you will love this tool.

Topstitch sewing-machine needles. These needles have an extra-large eye to accommodate thicker threads. I use these needles for rayon and embroidery threads when quilting or to sew decorative appliqué edges. The larger eye allows the threads to slide through without shredding. Use size 80/12 or 90/14 for the best results.

Value finder. If you are trying to determine the value of a fabric, place this red or green plastic rectangle in front of your eyes, and then look at the fabric. Red value finders work on all colors except red and yellow, while green value finders work on every color except green.

Water-soluble marking pen. These pens usually come in blue and are meant to be a temporary marking solution. Although not a good marker for quilting lines, sometimes these are the best tools to use for certain projects. Be sure to carefully and thoroughly wash out the blue lines after you are done, *before* you iron. If you iron on the marks made by these pens, they will become permanent. Washing will also remove any damaging chemicals from the fabric that may have been left by the pen.

Wonder Tape. Wrap a piece of this tape around your thread spools to tame loose ends. It is especially handy for shiny polyester and rayon threads, which always seem to unwind everywhere!

Wooden toothpicks. I use these inexpensive alternatives to an awl for turning under the seam allowance of freezer-paper appliqués as I stitch them down. They work better than a metal awl because they grab, rather than slide off, the fabric. I like the ones that have round, pointed ends and are square in the center where you grasp them.

Yardstick compass. Circles up to 72" in diameter can be made with this tool. It can be attached to a narrow plastic or metal ruler, or to a wooden yardstick. Screw the point onto the ruler at 0 and determine half the circle's size; then screw the lead carrier to that number on the ruler or yardstick. Keep your lead sharp for finer marked lines by sharpening it with a utility knife.

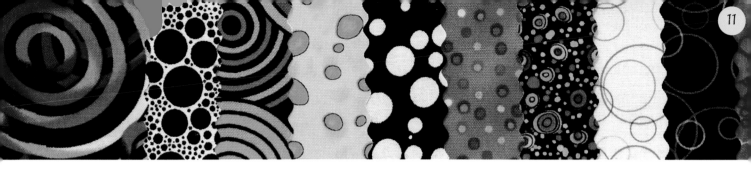

Fabrics

We are lucky to be quilting at a time when there are many wonderful fabric companies producing fabrics specifically for quilters. The variety of fabrics available is phenomenal, with something for everyone. As I worked on the quilts for this book, I was amazed at how many fabrics featured circles in the print. Medium circles, small circles, fat circles, doughnuts, and bubble prints were all available. It was difficult to choose!

Circle quilts can be made with any cotton fabric. Of course, the fabrics you choose will affect what your finished quilt will look like. This section will deal with how to use fabric design and color theory to make quilts that are special. Later, in "Embellishing Tools, Tips, and Techniques," beginning on page 21, we'll discuss how to use fabrics such as tulle and lamé to add special effects to your project.

Prints

Fabric choice can change the look of a quilt design from traditional to contemporary, or vice versa. If you prefer a traditional look, choose printed fabrics with regular, controlled designs. Paisleys and reproduction Civil War prints, as well as 1930s reproduction prints, are all examples of more traditional fabric choices. Examples of quilts that use traditional-style prints are "Nellie's Circle Four Patch" (page 31), "Patriotic Breezes" (page 65), and "Monkey's Fist" (page 35).

Batiks and hand-dyed or hand-painted fabrics will give your quilts a more contemporary look, as will black-and-white prints and bright prints. You can see examples of quilts that feature these fabrics in "Balls in the Air" (page 43), "Harvest Moon" (page 49), "Carnival" (page 53), and "Marbelous Marbles" (page 74).

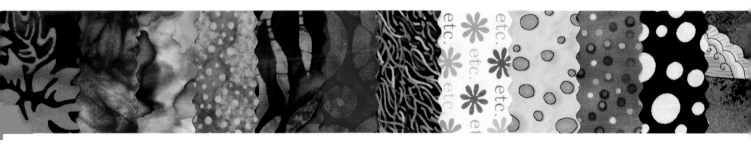

Contemporary prints

Traditional prints

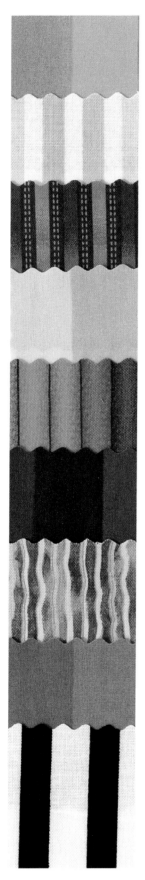

Ethnic prints are another good choice for contemporary-looking quilts. African, Australian, and Asian prints are readily available. "Circles of the Orient" (page 70) incorporates Asian prints.

Remember that the fabric you choose can totally change the feel of the quilt. Look at "Nellie's Circle Four Patch" (page 31) and compare it to "Circle Four Patch" (page 69). Both quilts are the same design, but they look completely different because of the fabrics chosen. The same is true for "Patriotic Breezes" (page 65), "Summer Breezes" (page 71), and "Easy as Pie" (page 71).

STRIPES

Some quilts in this book use stripes. Stripes are a wonderful way to add movement to a quilt, but they also have unique characteristics and challenges.

Striped fabric prints come in two variations: regular stripes and irregular stripes. Regular-striped fabrics have stripes that are all the same width or stripes of differing widths that are evenly spaced and have a planned repeat, such as a narrow stripe and a wide stripe that are repeated every other stripe. These types of stripes are easy to match. "Circles in the Attic" (page 39) is an example of a quilt where I used a regular-striped fabric.

Irregular-striped fabrics have stripes that vary in widths and have a random repeat. An irregular stripe might have small, medium, and large stripes in the same printed fabric. The color placement in an irregular stripe is also random, rather than a repeat pattern. Check out "Monkey's Fist II" (page 71) for an example of an irregular stripe and the first "Monkey's Fist" (page 35) for an irregular wavy stripe.

Matching stripes within the circles isn't necessary for any of the projects in this book, but a striped fabric was used in the background of "Circles in the Attic," which required matching. Matching the background stripes is easy when the stripes are matched and pinned before cutting out the blocks (refer to "A Perfect Match" on page 13). When sewing the blocks together, match the stripes once more, and pin to keep them in place.

Regular stripes (left) and irregular stripes (right)

A Perfect Match

An easy technique for matching a regular stripe is to cut the fabric in half lengthwise and then stack the halves right sides up, matching stripes of the same color. Pin along one or two stripes at regular intervals to keep the stripes from shifting as you cut out the pieces. You can use a rotary cutter to cut out strips for a quilt project, but *be careful* to move or avoid the pins when cutting. Pins really dull a rotary blade!

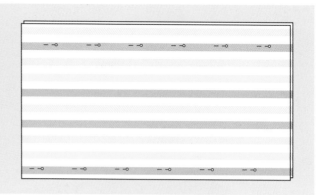

Irregular stripes are a challenge to match. This makes them perfect for "Monkey's Fist," a quilt where no matching is necessary. Even though both variations of the "Monkey's Fist" quilt use irregular stripes, the effect is very different. "Monkey's Fist" uses small wavy stripes, while "Monkey's Fist II" has a strong color change and stripes of multiple sizes.

Striped fabrics are printed with the stripes running either parallel or perpendicular to the selvage. The stripes I used in these projects are all printed parallel to the selvage edge. You may need more fabric for a particular project if you use a stripe printed perpendicular to the selvage. Fabrics with parallel stripes are more readily available than those with perpendicular stripes.

VALUE

It is important to pay attention to the value of a fabric when making your choices. Value refers to the lightness or darkness of a color and is usually divided into three increments: light, medium, and dark.

In the materials section of each project, value is often used to describe the fabrics needed. The best way to choose fabric for a given project is to lay out several fabrics next to each other and audition

Determining value can be challenging, because a fabric's value is directly related to the fabric(s) placed near it. A medium-value fabric can become a light if it is placed next to a dark fabric; a dark value can become medium if a darker fabric is placed next to it.

Prints in a variety of scales

them. This allows you to see how the fabrics relate to each other in regard to value. Make sure your fabrics follow the guidelines given. If the instructions call for a light and a medium, the fabric that is light needs to be lighter when placed next to the one of medium value. You should be able to see a definite change in value between the two fabrics.

If you have difficulty seeing value differences, a value finder can help you focus on the value rather than the color of a fabric. For more information on value finders, see "Tools" on page 8.

SCALE

Your quilt will be more interesting if you vary the scale of the prints you use. Scale refers to the size of the print and is usually broken into three divisions:

- Large-scale prints—motifs that are larger than 2"
- Medium-scale prints—motifs that range from ½" to 2"
- Small-scale prints—motifs less than ½"

Mixing a range of small-, medium-, and large-scale prints in your quilt is always more visually exciting than using prints of the same scale.

COLOR

Color is such an important aspect of quilting that whole books are written on the subject. I am only going to touch on a few highlights pertaining to the quilt projects in this book.

Colors are often described as "warm" or "cool." Warm colors are red violet, red, red orange, orange, and yellow. Cool colors are blue, blue green, green, violet, and blue violet. "Carnival" (page 53) uses these color descriptions to create a warm-color block and a cool-color block. These are then combined during the piecing process.

Warm colors give your quilts a rich, cozy feel. You'll find mostly warm colors used in "Harvest Moon" (page 49), "Batik Circles" (page 80), "Circles of the Orient" (page 70), and "Fowl Fantasy III" (page 70).

Sometimes using a tiny touch of a warm color in a mostly cool-color quilt can give the quilt added zing. Some examples of this technique can be found in "Circles in the Attic" (page 39), "Circle Four Patch" (page 69), "Sea Weeds" (page 73), and "Really, Really Broken Dishes (page 78).

Color strategies can be used to give a quilt a certain feel. For instance, a soft, comforting scrap quilt such as "Nellie's Circle Four Patch" (page 31) uses a variety of color, but the fabric prints are all similar in scale, value, and intensity. The intensity of a color describes how much white, gray, or black has been added to the color. The most intense colors are those on the outside edge of the color wheel. These are the purest form of each color. "Nellie's Circle Four Patch" uses grayed colors or less intense colors than "Circle Four Patch," and this causes each quilt to have a very different feel. One is soft and restful, while the other vibrates with pure color.

Another way to get an exciting, dramatic quilt is to pair complementary colors. Complementary colors are those that sit opposite each other on the color wheel, such as red and green, yellow and violet, and orange and blue. "Balls in the Air" (page 43), "Carnival" (page 53), "Clockworks" (page 59), "Monkey's Fist II" (page 71), and "Sun Spots" (page 75) use the complementary-color approach.

To tone down a quilt that is too vibrant, add some neutrals. Neutral colors are black, white, and beige. I used neutrals as backgrounds in "Balls in the Air" (page 43), "Carnival" (page 53), "Batik Circles" (page 80), and "Circles of the Orient" (page 70).

Color selection is a skill that improves with use. The more you play with color in your quilts the better your choices will be and the more interesting your quilts will become. Don't give up; it gets easier the more you do it!

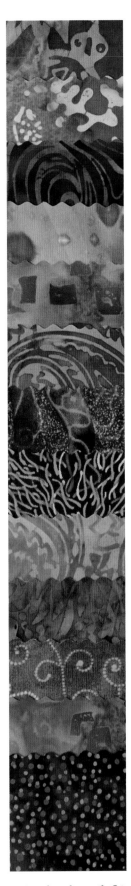

Cool colors (left) and warm colors (right)

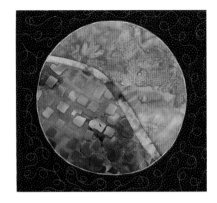

WORKING WITH CIRCLES

Circles aren't as easy to work with as straight lines, but with the techniques and hints I give you in this section, you'll be able to cut and appliqué them with ease in no time at all.

CUTTING TOOLS AND TECHNIQUES

A perfectly round appliqué begins with a well-cut circle. There are three tools you can use for cutting out circles: the Olfa Circle Cutter, a rotary cutter, or scissors. These tools also can be used to cut a doughnut, which is a circle with a smaller circle cut out of it. Following are the techniques for cutting circles and doughnuts. Be aware that before you cut out your circles, you will need to know which appliqué method you're going to use so you can determine the correct size circle to cut. Appliqué methods are covered later in this section.

Cutting with the Olfa Circle Cutter

The circle cutter has a rotary blade, just like your rotary cutter, but the ratchet mechanism allows it to turn in a circle. Using this tool eliminates the need to draw the circle first, making it the easiest and most efficient way to cut perfect fabric or paper circles. The cutter will make circles from 1⅞" to 8½", although I found that 3"-diameter circles were the smallest that I could cut satisfactorily.

To set the circle cutter, determine the diameter of the circle you want to cut. Divide this number in half. For the projects in this book, the number at which to set the blade is given in the project instructions. Loosen the screw above the point and place the tip of the point at 0 on the rotary mat and the cutter blade at the number you just determined. Tighten the screw. Your cutter is now ready to cut.

To cut, place the point into the fabric or paper you want to cut, making sure it is far enough into the fabric or paper so that you can make a complete rotation with the cutting arm. With one hand keeping the material flat on the cutting mat,

grasp the handle at the top of the cutter with your other hand and move in a clockwise motion with the blade against the material. Think "stirring soup." This is the motion you need to use. Be careful to keep the hand that is on the mat out of the way of the cutter blade!

Sometimes the cutter blade skips a spot, either because the downward pressure is not strong enough or because you are trying to cut through multiple seams, as with some of the quilts in this book. To remedy this problem, place the point back in the center of the circle and cut again carefully, trying to flatten the piece so the cutter can cut it. Another way to do this is to use a small rotary cutter and cut through the portion the circle cutter missed. Make sure you maintain the shape of the circle when doing this. If skipping is happening frequently, loosen the screw below the handle and move the handle either closer to the blade or farther away. Try both to see which works better for you.

Practice makes a big difference with this tool. Keep trying and you will get better and better. Remember the first time you used a rotary cutter? Now you are a whiz at it.

Tips for Circle Cutter Use
• Cut through one layer at a time.
• Keep the rotary blade in the circle cutter clean by brushing it with a sewing-machine lint brush or a cotton swab. Because the blade is so small, it fills up quickly with lint from your fabrics and this lint interferes with the cutting action.
• Protect your hands and feet by always covering the blade and point with their respective safety covers when the cutter is not in use.

Cutting with a Rotary Cutter or Scissors
If you use either of these tools, you will first need to draw a circle of the desired size onto the fabric or paper. A compass will give you the most accurate results.

To set the compass, determine the diameter of the circle you want to cut. Divide this number in half and set the compass at this number. For the projects in this book, the compass setting is given in the project instructions. To get nice, round circles, cut out the circles on the drawn line with scissors or with an 18 mm rotary cutter. The tiny blade cuts terrific circles, like drawing with a pencil. The disadvantage to using this cutter is that you can only cut one or two layers of fabric or paper at a time.

Freezer-Paper Circles
To cut multiple circles for freezer-paper appliqué, press four layers of freezer paper together, paper sides up, with a *warm*, not hot, dry iron. Cut out the circles, and then gently peel apart the freezer-paper shapes.

Cutting a Doughnut
For some of the projects in this book, you will cut a smaller circle from the center of a larger circle to create a doughnut. Cut the larger circle first, following the cutting instructions for one of the cutting tools described previously. Place the point of the compass or circle cutter at the center point of the circle, and then cut out the inner circle to

create the hole. You can see examples of dough-nuts in "Harvest Moon" (page 49) and "Carnival" (page 53).

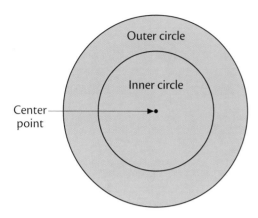

CENTERING A CIRCLE

Once your circles are cut, you're going to appliqué them to the background fabric. Most of the quilts in this book center the circle in a square and then stitch it in place. The easiest way to center your circle is to fold the square in half horizontally and then in half vertically. Finger-press the folds made in the center of the square and then unfold it. The point at which the fold lines intersect is the center.

Now you need to find the center of the circle. If you cut your circle with the circle cutter or used a compass to mark a circle, your fabric will have a hole in the center where the point of the tool rested. Hold your circle up to the light to find the hole. If the hole hides, fold your circle in quarters like you did with the square and finger-press the folds. Open up the circle to the right side and insert a pin through the intersecting point. Then insert the pin through the intersection of the folds in the center of your square, making your pin stand up perpendicular to the surface. I do this on my pressing mat or ironing board. Having the pin in the center and upright allows you to rotate your circle into the position where you want it while keeping it centered in the square. When you're happy with the placement, pin your centered circle in place. You are ready to appliqué.

APPLIQUÉ METHODS

Appliqué is the process of attaching a shape that you cut from one fabric to a larger piece of another fabric. There are several ways to do this, but I prefer the following two methods.

Fusible-Web Appliqué

For this method, you fuse the shape to the background fabric and then add stitching around the edges of the appliqué to permanently secure it. There are many different fusible webs on the market, but my favorite is regular Wonder-Under, a paper-backed transfer web manufactured by Pellon. This was one of the first fusible webs developed and I still prefer it for the techniques I use. It is light enough to sew or quilt through and does not show through thin fabrics like batiks. If you use another type of fusible product, make sure it can be stitched through (avoid anything labeled as "heavy"), and always follow the manufacturer's instructions. Following are general instructions for the fusible-web method. Pressing times reflect those I use for Wonder-Under, which could be different from other fusible webs.

1. Cut a piece of fusible web the size of the fabric to which you are going to adhere it. Place the piece on the appliqué fabric with the glue side against the wrong side of the fabric and the paper side facing up. Using a hot, dry iron, press the web in place, holding it in each spot for five seconds until the entire piece has been fused. Bubbles often show up on the right side of batiks, so for these fabrics I also press from the right side, carefully working from the center toward the outer edges to flatten the fabric.

2. From the fused fabric, cut out the circle in the size specified in the project instructions, using one of the cutting methods described earlier.

3. Remove the paper backing from the wrong side of the circle and lay it in place on the background piece. Temporarily tack down the circle by lightly pressing it with the iron. Cover the circle with a damp pressing cloth and press it in place with an iron set on wool for 10 seconds. Let the piece cool and then check the bond. If any portion of the circle has not adhered to the fabric, repeat the fusing process until it is fully bonded.

4. To permanently attach the fused circle to the background, machine stitch it in place. Set your machine for a zigzag stitch and use a decorative thread or monofilament to stitch around the edges. Using decorative thread will make the edges of the appliqué an important part of the design. Change the width of the zigzag stitch for different looks, or try variegated thread for an edge that changes colors around the circle. Monofilament is nearly invisible and when used with a narrow zigzag stitch can give the look of hand appliqué.

For a flat, smooth satin stitch, pin a tear-away stabilizer to the wrong side of the background fabric under the appliqué when stitching with the zigzag stitch. When you're finished stitching, tear away the stabilizer. For more ideas about edge finishes for your fusible appliqués, refer to "Embellishing Tools, Tips, and Techniques" on page 21.

Protective Paper

Save the paper backing from used fusible web, especially the larger pieces. The paper is great for protecting your iron so that the fusible-web glue doesn't melt onto it. Once you have these papers you will find all kinds of uses for them. Any time you want to adhere something without getting glue on your iron, it is the perfect thing to use.

Freezer-Paper Appliqué

With freezer-paper appliqué, the edges of the circles are turned under and then machine stitched in place. A freezer-paper circle that is cut the size of the finished circle is used to shape the fabric circle.

1. Cut the number of circles from freezer paper in the size instructed for your project, using one of the cutting methods described previously.

2. Lay the freezer-paper circles, coated (shiny) side down, on the wrong side of the appliqué fabrics. If you are cutting more than one circle from the same fabric, leave at least ¾" between shapes. Press the circles in place with a dry iron set on permanent press. Press each circle for about five seconds or until it sticks to the fabric. Because the bond is temporary, manipulating the fabric too much can cause the freezer paper to peel away from the fabric. If this happens, just press the circle in place again. This can be done several times if necessary.

3. Cut out the fabric circles ⅜" larger than the freezer-paper circles. If you're cutting with the circle cutter, place the point in the same hole you made when you cut the freezer-paper circle.

4. With the freezer-paper side up, press the seam allowance over the edge of the freezer-paper circle with the tip of the iron, being careful not to bend the freezer paper. You want to keep a nice round circle with no flat sides.

5. Place the appliqué in the desired location on the background fabric and pin it in place.

6. Set your sewing machine for a narrow zigzag stitch and a short stitch length. Thread your machine with monofilament in the top and a neutral color in the bobbin. Place the appliqué under the needle and prepare to stitch. Using a wooden toothpick or an awl, tuck a little bit of the seam allowance in front of the needle securely under the appliqué. Pressing under the seam allowance with the iron helps shape the circle but the creases tend to fall out as you stitch, and this step is necessary for a nice round circle. The distance you will be able to tuck under will change with the size of the circle. For larger circles, you can tuck under about 1½" at a time, but for smaller circles, ½" will be all you can tuck without getting points or flat sides. Stitch the portion you tucked under. You want one side of the stitch to fall off the circle and into the background and the other side to fall on the circle. I usually sew with the circle to the left of the needle; that way my "zig" is in the circle and the "zag" falls off the edge. Make sure the background fabric remains flat and the appliqué does not move as you stitch. If your bobbin thread shows on the top of the fabric, reduce the thread tension. Continue tucking under and stitching a small portion at a time until you reach the beginning of your stitches. Overlap the stitching at the end by slightly less than ¼".

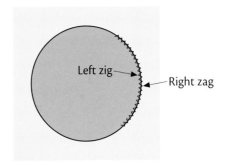

Left zig   Right zag

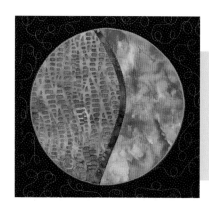

Hot Tip

If you use monofilament to stitch your appliqués, be careful to set your iron on the polyester setting and no higher. You don't want your thread to melt! Also, avoid using commercial dryers, which are too hot for monofilament thread and polyester battings.

7. After the appliqué is stitched to the background, flip the piece over and cut a tiny hole in the fabric behind the circle, about ¼" inside the edge. Pull the fabric up and cut away the background fabric behind the circle, leaving a ⅜" seam allowance. The freezer paper is still in place and it helps prevent you from cutting your appliqué circle, but be careful that you don't snip into the circle fabric when doing this step. Save these background circles and use them in another circle quilt. Check out the two sister quilts, "Marbelous Marbles" on page 74 and "Glass Bubbles" on page 77. I created "Marbelous Marbles" first and used some of the circles cut from behind the appliqués in "Glass Bubbles."

8. Remove the freezer paper from behind the appliqué. Pull an edge of the appliqué away from the freezer paper to release a portion, and then insert your fingers or the eraser side of a pencil and release the rest of the freezer paper from the back of the circle. My favorite tool for this process is an unused chopstick. Tear the freezer paper away from the stitched line. It should tear away relatively easily because the stitching perforated the freezer paper. A very small amount of freezer paper will remain under the zigzag stitching, but this isn't a problem. The chopstick method works especially well on small circles where you can't fit your fingers between the appliqué and the freezer paper.

EMBELLISHING TOOLS, TIPS, AND TECHNIQUES

The embellishments used on a quilt can make it either a showstopper or an eyesore.

When determining how much embellishment to use, there is a fine line between enough and too much. You have to carefully consider whether the embellishments make sense with the rest of the piece. Embellishments need to relate to all the other parts of the quilt, from the design, to the appliqué technique, to the quilting. Every part of the quilt needs to work with each other or one will overwhelm the rest. This is difficult because each step is done separately and the end result is not visible until we get there! Often, as I work on one step I am thinking about the next, and when I reach that step I have already decided what I want to try. I say "try," because I do not always end up doing what I thought I was going to. Once you lay the threads on the quilt to audition them, sometimes what you thought would be fabulous is wrong for the piece and you have to adjust your plan.

There are a huge number of ways to embellish your quilt. I have only been able to include a few here, but whole books are devoted to beading and embellishment techniques. Check out "Resources" on page 95 for a listing of places to purchase embellishment supplies and books. I have also tried to give you tips and tricks for working with the embellishments, from tools to the embellishments themselves. Each type of embellishment has certain characteristics that make it special but can also make it difficult to work with. Hopefully my tips will help to make your adventure in embellishing your quilt a success.

EMBELLISHING WITH THREAD

There are hundreds of wonderful threads available to quilters today, and manufacturers are constantly striving to develop threads that are easy to use for a variety of sewing and quilting purposes. Embroidery machines have caused the thread market to explode with a multitude of specialty threads. I have included some of the manufacturers and retail outlets for threads and other embellishments in "Resources," but there are many more that I did not have space to include.

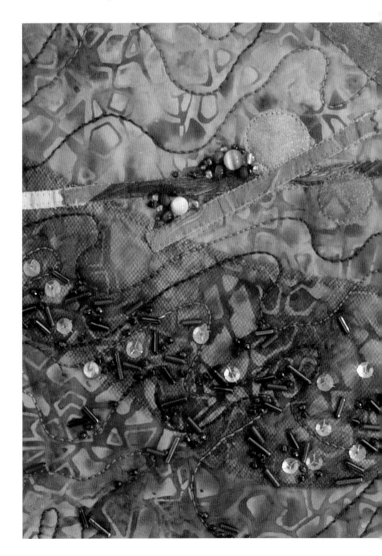

Each type of thread has its own characteristics, so you'll need to experiment with needle size and machine settings to achieve the desired look. I've worked with rayon, polyester, and heavy threads a lot over the years, so you may find the following information helpful when working with these threads.

Rayon and Polyester Threads

The sheen on rayon and polyester thread makes them slippery and slick, which can cause a few problems. Often these threads come in larger cones or spools and if placed in an upright or vertical position, the slippery thread falls off the spool in rings of loose thread. There are two ways to deal with this. The first is to place the thread in your sewing machine horizontally, if your machine has that capability. If your machine does not have a horizontal spool pin, then use a thread stand. A thread stand usually has a heavy plastic base wider than the thread cone, a metal pin to put the cone on, and a tall metal thread guide that positions your thread for feeding into your sewing machine. Place the stand behind the sewing machine, carry the thread over the top of the machine to the first thread guide, and thread normally.

Another common problem with fine shiny threads is that the thread catches on the cut on the end of the spool when sewing, causing immediate tension problems and thread breakage. This is easily resolved by placing the spool on the pin with the cut in the spool facing the opposite direction from the threading of the sewing machine. Usually this means that the end with the cut goes on the spool pin first.

Shiny rayon threads also tend to shred when you work with them at a high sewing-machine speed. This can be corrected by using a product called Sewer's Aid on the thread before threading your machine. For specifics on the use of Sewer's Aid and cautionary remarks, see the product information in "Tools" on page 8. Another solution to shredding problems is to change the size or the type of sewing-machine needle you are using. I often use topstitch needles with rayon thread, because the larger, longer eye of the needle allows the thread more room to move and results in less shredding. Sew slower when doing decorative

Size Wise

Thread size is listed on the end or edge of the spool, with smaller numbers being thicker thread and larger numbers being finer thread. For instance, size 12 is a heavy embroidery thread and size 40 is a fine (thin) thread. Rayon threads often come in size 40. As a general guideline, use a larger needle for thicker threads and a smaller needle for thinner threads. More information on needle sizes can be found on pages 8–10.

Threads of a Different Color

When using a variegated thread, use the same thread in the top and bobbin of the sewing machine. Pull out the bobbin thread until it matches the color that is just coming through the eye of the needle. This helps hide the bobbin thread if it peeks through to the top of the quilt.

stitching with these shiny threads, allowing them time to slide through the needle and form a stitch. This is also true when quilting with these threads.

Heavy Threads

When using a heavy thread like pearl cotton, you have to make adjustments to your sewing machine to make it work smoothly. Reduce the thread tension considerably when using heavy threads and use a larger needle. I often use a size 90 topstitch needle, but you might even consider a size 100. The goal is to use the smallest needle that works consistently and doesn't break the thread. A normal-weight thread usually works in the bobbin.

For the best results when sewing, sew slowly and use a stabilizer under the fabric. Sew around the circle to the beginning and try to land the needle in the hole of the first stitch you made. Cut the threads, leaving a 3" tail. Thread the tails into the eye of an embroidery needle and pull them to the back of the quilt top. Sometimes with heavy thread you can tug on the bobbin thread and it will pull a loop of the top thread to the back. Grab the loop and pull the tail all the way through to the back. Tie the top and bobbin thread tails together and clip to within ¼" of the quilt. When tying threads together, check the right side of the quilt top to make sure the bobbin threads are not showing.

In "Carnival" (page 53), I embellished circle edges with a satin stitch. The stitch length is short, causing the stitches to lie next to each other and form a solid line of decorative stitching. Holographic, neon, and variegated threads give this quilt a festive feel. The thread colors echo the colors of the fabric they are stitched on. You could use a thread that contrasts with the fabric, and then the stitching would appear as a visible line rather than as part of the shape.

In "Clockworks" (page 59), I used a hand-dyed pearl cotton to stitch the outside edges of the gears. On the larger gears, I used the widest-width zigzag and adjusted the stitch length to yield a longer stitch rather than the short stitch length used for a satin stitch. The smaller gears use a zigzag width that is one full size down.

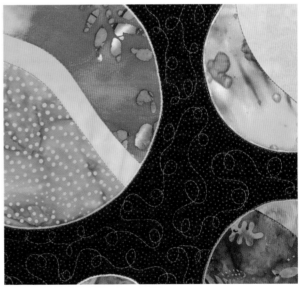

Another quilt that uses a heavy thread and a zig-zag stitch is "Marbelous Marbles" (page 74). Here, the zigzag width is smaller and the outside "zag" follows the edge of the circle, which is in con-trast to "Clockworks" (above right), where the wide zigzag line is centered over the edge of the appliquéd gear. The smaller zigzag emphasizes the edge of the circle and adds a dimensional quality to the appliqué.

Zigzag stitching accents fused appliqués in "Balls in the Air" (page 43). I chose a narrow zigzag rather than a wide one, because I wanted just a touch of color at the edge of the circle to unify the colors of the piecing. This way, the viewer sees a circle rather than the shapes within the circle.

Using blue tulle rescued "Summer Breezes" (page 71), providing much-needed contrast within the blocks.

Fused lamé appliqués in "Clockworks" (page 59)

EMBELLISHING WITH DECORATIVE FABRICS

Decorative fabrics are terrific for adding a touch of glitz or modifying a color on your quilt. There are several specialty fabrics that I use in my quilts, but it is important to understand their characteristics before you use them.

I often use tulle to add a shadow or to adjust a color slightly. Because tulle is a netting, or an open-meshed fabric, the quilt top shows through the holes and the tulle subtly adds color and texture to the piece. Tulle and other nettings can also add sparkle, depending on the fabric chosen. There are nettings with designs printed on them, some of which are flocked, as well as plain nettings. But remember, the more design the netting has, the less transparent it becomes.

Working with tulle has its advantages and disadvantages. One advantage is that tulle won't fray along cut edges. This means you can lay a piece of tulle where you want it, stitch it down, and cut the edges near the stitched line without worrying about frayed edges later. Because it is made of nylon, tulle has a very low melting point. It can only be ironed with a slightly warm iron; anything hotter than that melts it. As a result, tulle is not a good choice for a quilt that needs to be washed often. It is a delicate fabric that does not deal well with abrasion or the heat of a machine dryer.

Another decorative fabric that is more opaque than tulle but still has a transparent quality is organza. This fabric works great for bubbles because it adds sheen and yet is semitransparent. Polyester organza, unlike tulle, can be ironed with a hotter iron, but it frays at the cut edges. Once again the characteristics of the fabric do not lend themselves to machine washing and drying.

If you want to add glitz to your project, lamé is a wonderful choice. Lamé comes in several colors, all with a metallic quality. Lamé is made with nylon or cotton warp threads and metal weft threads. The stronger warp threads hold the fragile metal threads in place and give the fabric a little strength without adding any color. Lamé is an extremely shiny, very lightweight fabric, and it adds a precious quality to a quilt top, but it is another fabric that needs special treatment. It is not very washable

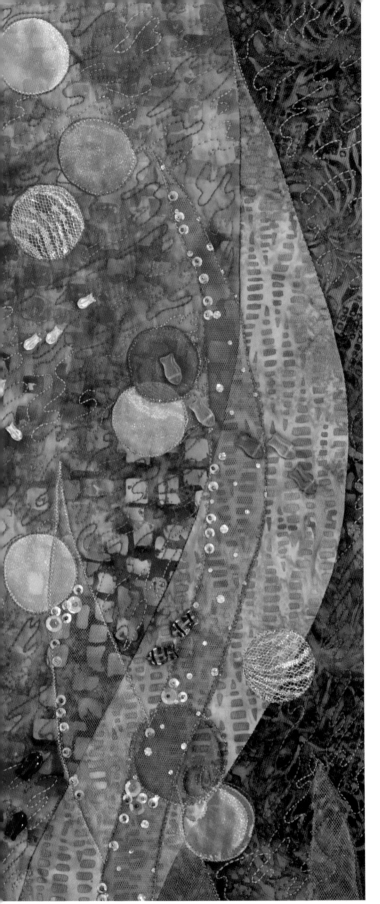

and the nylon warp threads make it susceptible to melting, so only a very cool iron can be used. There is also a possibility that detergent may cause the metallic threads to tarnish or become dull. Because the weave structure is looser, lamé needs to be stabilized before using it in a quilt. Fuse a woven or knit interfacing to the wrong side of the lamé before using. Pick an interfacing that has a low fusing temperature requirement to accommodate the nylon warp threads in the lamé. The fused interfacing helps counteract fraying and keeps the edges stable so that they don't stretch out of shape. Interfaced lamé can also be fused to paper-backed fusible web and used in fused appliqué techniques.

EMBELLISHING WITH BEADS

A whole world of beads is available, and beads are as addictive as fabric for many of us. Beads come in shiny or matte forms, in all different sizes and shapes, and are made with everything from glass to plastic to natural products such as wood, bone, horn, and stone.

Choosing the perfect bead for your embellishment needs is often daunting when there is such a huge array of choices. I select beads based on the theme of a project and by auditioning the beads on the actual quilt top to see how the colors work and how the beads catch the light. Be aware that the type of light—fluorescent, natural, or incandescent—makes a difference in the color and reflective quality of certain beads. These characteristics can change in different lighting situations. Make your choices in the light where you anticipate the piece will hang.

A quilt with a carnival theme can make use of beads with a lot of shiny, light-reflective qualities. Quilts with a more natural theme may look best embellished with beads made from a natural source, such as shell or stone. "Glass Bubbles" on page 77 uses a mixture of natural and glass beads, as well as sequins and matte and shiny bugle beads. The characteristics of beads, their delicacy, hardness, and the fact that they are added by hand make

I used organza for the small bubbles, appliquéing them to "Sea Weeds" (page 73) with a transparent thread and a narrow zigzag stitch.

Beading used in "Clockworks" (page 59)

them especially good for wall quilts, art quilts, or wearable art.

You can add beads before or after the quilt top is quilted. Your choice depends upon the look you are attempting to achieve. Adding the beads to the quilt top *before* it is layered and quilted means you have to avoid the beads when you quilt. If you are machine quilting you can only stitch ¼", the width of the presser foot, from the bead. This means that the beads will lie on the puffier, raised part of the

quilt rather than the indented part, which is where the quilting stitches are. If you want your beads to follow a quilted line or be in the valley that the quilting forms, you have to add the beads *after* you quilt. Both techniques work equally well. The main difference in actually attaching the beads is where the knots and carrying stitches lie. When you attach the beads first, before quilting, the knots and carrying threads lie on the back of the quilt top. Once you layer the quilt, these will never be seen. It is also easier to manipulate the fabric of a quilt top than the fabric of a fully quilted quilt because there is less bulk to work around. This becomes more of an issue the larger the quilt is. I usually attach the beads after quilting, and the knots and carrying stitches are buried between the layers of the quilt. Refer to "Making and Using the Quilter's Knot" (page 29).

Beading Tools

Beaded embellishment requires very few specialized tools. The main differences are the threads and needles used. The two threads I use for adding most beads to a quilt are Nymo and C-Lon. Both of these threads are made of nylon, making them very strong. Nymo has flat nylon filaments, while C-Lon is made of twisted nylon filaments. C-Lon comes in a wide range of colors, which is an advantage for beading on fabric. Both C-Lon and Nymo can be found in beading and craft stores. I have also included some Internet merchants in "Resources" on page 95 in case you can't find them locally. Another thread I use, especially when attaching bugle beads, is Conso upholstery thread. This is a heavy-duty nylon thread that resists abrasion, which is why I use it for cut beads such as bugles. Conso is a twisted filament that has a finish applied to it, making it very similar to hand quilting thread in appearance.

Color Conscious

Always test your thread color on a bead, especially if you are working with transparent beads. The thread color shows through the bead and can change the bead's appearance.

My favorite needle for sewing beads to fabric is a size 10 appliqué needle. It is fine enough to fit through most beads and is long enough to go through the bead and fabric. Sometimes I add a string of beads as a fringe or dangling from the center of a piece, and for these applications I use a beading needle. A beading needle is very fine and long. It can be loaded with lots of beads, which is good for fringe-type applications. I have not incorporated this technique in any of the quilts in this book, but you might like to try it. The beading needle is so fine that it tends to bend and break, so it is not a good choice for sewing beads to fabric.

Beading Stitches and Techniques

There are as many ways to sew beads onto fabric as there are bead embroiderers. You may see a different beading technique in another book, but the ones covered here are the ones I like to use. For all the stitches, use an appliqué needle threaded with an 18" to 20" length of beading thread. Knot one end with a quilter's knot (see page 29), letting the other end hang free so that you are stitching with a single thread.

Security Stitch. This is the stitch you use to sew on individual beads, whether they are in groups or spaced apart. One of my favorite techniques is to make "bead soup." To make "bead soup," mix a variety of different bead sizes, shapes, sheens, and colors together, and then sew them in one area of the quilt. Even though the beads are close together, they must be sewn on individually. When sewing on individual beads, I use a security stitch. Using this stitch ensures that if one bead should become loose and fall off, only a couple of others will follow instead of every single one.

With the threaded needle, come up through the fabric at A. Take a tiny stitch, going down at B and coming up again at A. This makes a security stitch that hides under the bead and keeps the bead secure if the knot comes apart. Put a bead on the threaded needle and go down at B. Repeat the last step so that you are going through the bead a total

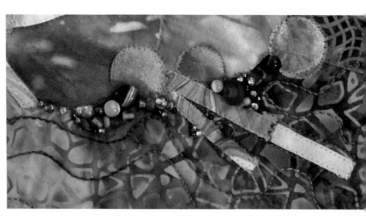

Different sizes and shapes of beads in a group are best sewn on with a security stitch. The grouping here is part of "Glass Bubbles" (page 77).

of two times. Going through a bead twice makes the bead stand up; otherwise it tends to fall over and the hole shows.

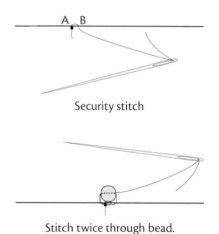

Security stitch

Stitch twice through bead.

The next two beads will be sewn on without the security stitch. Just add the bead and go through the hole twice. Every third bead, I sew a security stitch before adding the bead. When all the beads have been added in the area you are stitching, knot your thread on the back of your fabric or knot and bury the knot as instructed in "Making and Using the Quilter's Knot."

Beaded Backstitch. Sometimes I want to add a line of beads. The line can be straight or curved, long or short. The stitch I use in this situation is called the beaded backstitch. In the beaded backstitch there is an automatic security stitch built into the stitch.

With the threaded needle, come up through the fabric, put three beads on the thread, and lay in a row on the fabric, go down after the last bead, making sure the beads lie flat on the fabric. Come up between the last two beads in the group and go through the hole of the last bead. Add three more beads to the needle before taking another backstitch by going down after the last bead and coming up between the last two beads as before. Continue in the same manner, taking a backstitch at every third bead. Knot your thread on the back of your fabric, or knot and bury the knot as instructed in "Making and Using the Quilter's Knot."

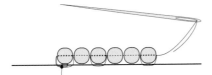

Take a backstitch every third bead.

Attaching Bugle Beads. Bugle beads are hollow glass tubes cut to different sizes. Depending on the quality of the bead, the cut ends will be burnished smooth or left sharp. Sharp ends will, of course, wear at your thread and eventually cut through it. Upholstery thread is stronger than other threads, but the sharp edges can still wear it down. The best method of attaching bugle beads to fabric is to add a round seed bead to each end of the bugle bead. This way the thread turns and goes into the fabric after going through the smooth hole of the seed bead, preventing the wear it would get from rubbing across the end of the bugle bead.

With a threaded needle come up at A. Add a seed bead, a bugle bead, and then another seed bead to the needle and go down at B; repeat to add as many beads as desired. You can also add a small security stitch under the beads periodically, if desired. When finished, knot your thread on the back of your fabric, or knot and bury the knot as instructed in "Making and Using the Quilter's Knot."

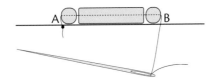

Embellishing with Sequins

Sequins are a fun way to add some glitz to a quilt. Here are just a couple of methods of sewing sequins to fabric.

Using a decorative thread, come up in the center of the sequin, go down next to the outer edge, come up in the center again, and go down next to the outer edge in a different location. This can be done two, three, or four times, depending on where you place the needle along the outer edge and the look you desire.

Another fun way to attach sequins that adds a three-dimensional quality is to use seed beads, alone or with bugle beads. Use your imagination to create many variations using this method. With a threaded needle, come up through the hole in the sequin, add a seed bead to the needle, and then go down through the hole in the sequin. The seed bead holds the sequin in place. Seed beads smaller than the sequin allow more of the sequin to show, while larger beads hide the sequin. Other variations with bugle beads and multiple sequins are shown below. When you are finished stitching, knot your thread on the back of your fabric, or knot and bury the knot as instructed in "Making and Using the Quilter's Knot."

Making and Using the Quilter's Knot

The quilter's knot is used by hand quilters to begin and end a line of quilting. It also works very well for securing a line of beads or sequins after quilting.

To make a quilter's knot:

1. Thread the needle, leaving a short tail and a long tail. Run the long thread tail between your left forefinger and thumb until you reach the end of the thread. Grasp this thread end between the thumb and forefinger of your left hand with the end of the thread pointing down. (Left-handers need to reverse these instructions.)

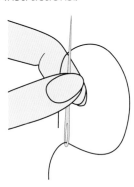

2. Place the threaded needle, point up, in your left hand between your forefinger and thumb. Grasp the trailing thread and wrap it around the needle point one or two times, pinching the thread wrap on the needle between your left forefinger and thumb. Pull the needle point up and out of your finger and thumb while still retaining a gentle hold on the thread. The thread will pull through the loose loops and a knot will form at the end of the thread. Tighten the knot with your fingers.

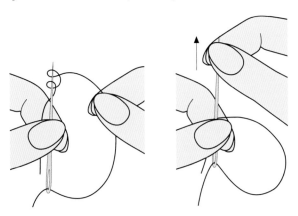

3. To begin a stitched or beaded line with a quilter's knot, place the point of the needle about ¼" from the point where you want to start. Bring the needle through the fabric at the point where you want your stitching to begin. Pull the thread through and give a gentle tug to pull the knot through the first hole and between the layers of the quilt. Don't pull too hard or you will pull it all the way through both holes and you'll have to start again!

To end a stitched or beaded line with a quilter's knot, finish stitching and leave enough thread to form a knot, about 5" or so. Holding the thread out with your left hand, turn the point of the needle back toward your line of stitching and wrap the thread you are holding around the point twice. Holding on to the loops on the needle, pull the thread back around and under the needle once. Put the needle point with the thread wrapped around it into the fabric at the end of your last stitch, and carry the needle between the layers of the quilt, going the opposite direction from your stitching, for approximately ¼" before coming up through the top fabric. Pull the thread gently until you hear the knot pop as it enters the batting layer. Cut the thread ends even with the fabric.

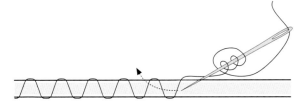

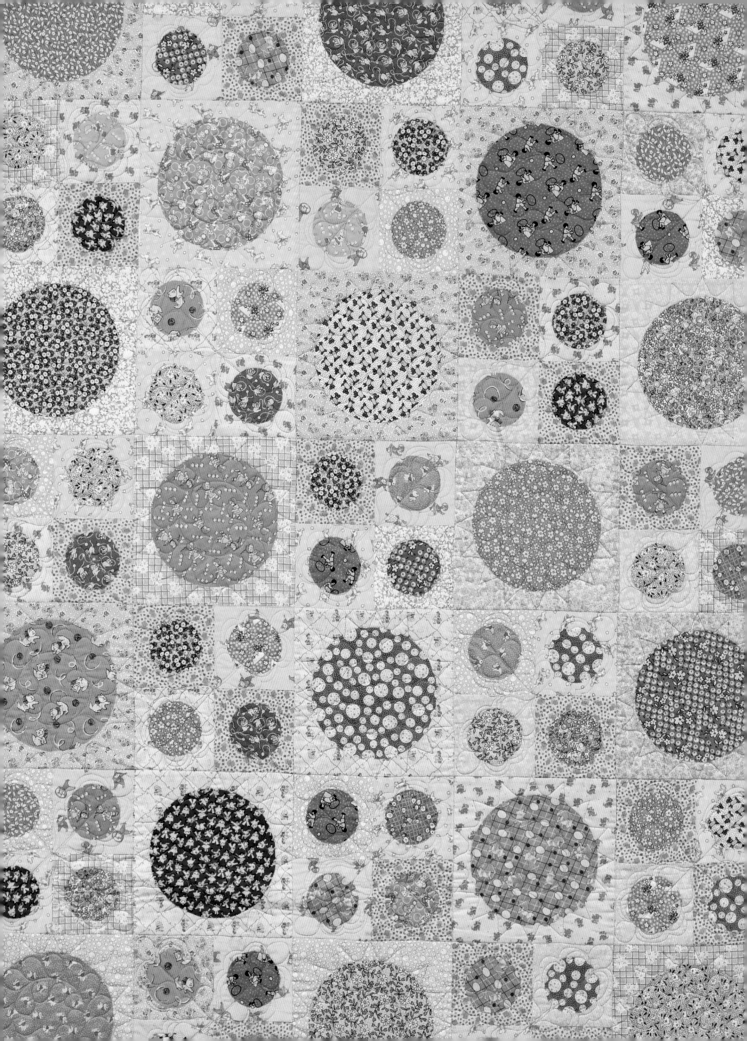

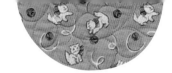

Nellie's Circle Four Patch

For the old-fashioned look of a scrap quilt, use a wide variety of prints. Sew circles to squares without a plan; just pick two fabrics that you like together and appliqué. This quilt was named in memory of my Grandmother Nellie.

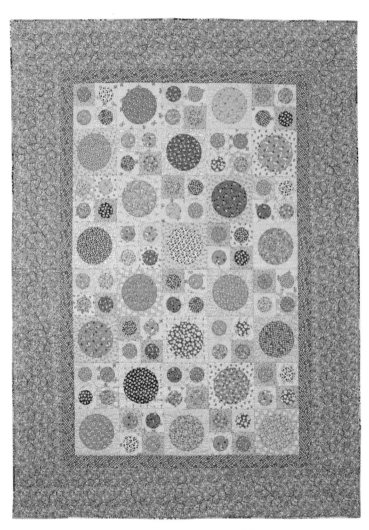

Pieced by Leigh E. McDonald, 2005;
quilted by Linda Cline, The Feathered Fern

Skill Level: Beginner/Intermediate
Finished Quilt Size: 69½" x 96½"
Finished Block Size: 9" x 9"

MATERIALS

All yardages are based on 42"-wide fabric.

3½ yards *total* of assorted light and medium print scraps for block backgrounds

2½ yards of lavender print for outer border

2 yards *total* of assorted medium and dark print scraps for block circle appliqués

⅔ yard of light blue print for inner border

⅔ yard of fabric for binding (or see tip for scrappy binding on page 33)

6½ yards of fabric for backing (pieced lengthwise)

78" x 105" piece of batting

CUTTING

All measurements include ¼"-wide seam allowances. Cut all strips across the width of the fabric.

From the assorted light and medium print scraps, cut a *total* of:
20 squares, 9½" x 9½"
80 squares, 5" x 5"

From the assorted medium and dark print scraps, cut a *total* of:
20 squares, 8" x 8"
80 squares, 4" x 4"

From the light blue print, cut:
7 strips, 3" wide

From the lavender print, cut:
8 strips, 10" wide

From the binding fabric, cut:
10 strips, 2" wide

MAKING THE BLOCKS

1. Refer to "Working with Circles" on page 16 to determine your preferred appliqué method, and then cut out the circle appliqués from the medium and dark print squares. *For fusible appliqué*, use a compass or circle cutter set at 3½" to make a 7"-diameter circle from each 8" square. Use a compass or circle cutter set at 1½" and make a 3"-diameter circle from each 4" square. *For freezer-paper appliqué*, use the same compass/circle cutter settings as for fusible appliqué to make circle templates from freezer paper. Make 20 that are 7" in diameter and 80 that are 3" in diameter. Press the 7"-diameter circles onto the 8" squares and the 3"-diameter circles onto the 4" squares, and then use a rotary cutter, scissors, or circle cutter to cut out the fabric circles ⅜" larger than the freezer-paper circles.

2. Using the appliqué method you selected in step 1, appliqué each large circle to a light or medium print 9½" square, centering the circle in the square. Repeat with the small circles and the light or medium print 5" squares.

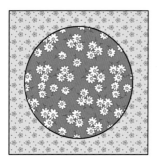

Make 20.

Make 80.

Mix It Up!

For a scrappy look, just grab a circle and a square. The visual effect is more random and spontaneous than assigning color placements in advance.

3. Sew four 5" squares together to make a Four Patch block, matching the edges and seams. Mix up the background and circle fabrics for each block as much as possible. Press the seam allowances as indicated. Repeat to make a total of 20 blocks.

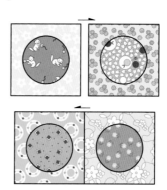

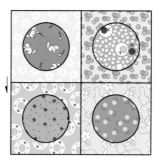

Make 20.

ASSEMBLING THE QUILT TOP

1. Refer to the quilt assembly diagram at right to arrange the blocks into eight horizontal rows of five blocks each, alternating the placement of the blocks in each row and from row to row.

2. Sew the blocks in each row together. Press the seam allowances in opposite directions from row to row.

3. Sew the rows together, matching edges and seams. Press the seam allowances in one direction.

4. Carefully square up the quilt top, using a square ruler for the corners and a long ruler and rotary cutter for the sides. Your quilt center is done!

ADDING THE BORDERS

For general instructions on measuring and sewing borders, refer to "Adding Borders" on page 91.

1. Sew two light blue strips together end to end. Repeat to make one additional pieced strip. Measure the quilt top for the side borders. Trim the pieced strips to the length measured, and sew them to the sides of the quilt top. Press the seam allowances toward the border strips.

2. Cut one of the remaining light blue strips in half crosswise. Sew one half to the end of each of the remaining full-length light blue strips. Measure the quilt top for the top and bottom borders. Trim the pieced strips to the length measured, and sew them to the top and bottom of the quilt top. Press the seam allowances toward the border strips.

3. Sew two lavender print strips together end to end. Repeat to make a total of four pieced strips. Trim and then sew the pieced strips to the quilt top in the same manner as the inner border, pressing the seam allowances toward the outer-border strips.

FINISHING THE QUILT

Referring to "Basic Quiltmaking Techniques," beginning on page 90, layer the quilt top with batting and backing fabric, and baste the layers together. Quilt as desired. Quilting around the circles in this quilt will really make them pop! See "Quilting Ideas" on page 81 for more quilting designs and suggestions. Bind the edges with the 2"-wide binding strips.

Scrap-Happy Binding

A scrappy binding is a great way to continue the feel of this quilt. Using your leftover circle fabrics, cut 2"-wide strips of varying lengths and sew them together end to end into one long piece. You will need a strip approximately 350" long. Apply the binding as usual.

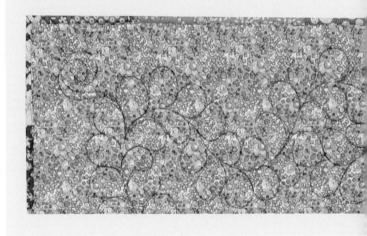

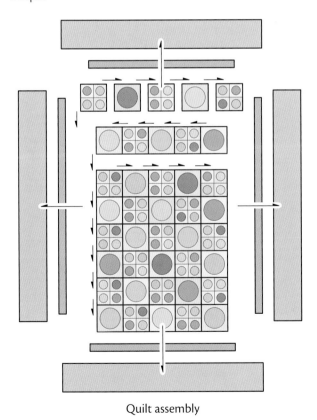

Quilt assembly

MONKEY'S FIST

The circles in this wall hanging remind me of the monkey's fist knot that we used to tie in Girl Scouts. Check out "Monkey's Fist II" on page 71 in the "Gallery" for a slightly different variation.

By Leigh E. McDonald, 2005

Skill Level: Beginner/Intermediate
Finished Quilt Size: 45½" x 56½"
Finished Block Size: 10" x 10"

MATERIALS

All yardages are based on 42"-wide fabric.

1⅔ yards of striped print for circle appliqués and binding

1⅓ yards of cream print for block backgrounds

1⅛ yards of large-scale purple print for outer border

⅝ yard of lavender print for sashing and inner border

¼ yard of lime green print for sashing and border cornerstones

3⅓ yards of fabric for backing (pieced crosswise)

54" x 65" piece of batting

CUTTING

All measurements include ¼"-wide seam allowances. Cut all strips across the width of the fabric.

From the striped print, cut:
6 strips, 2" wide
12 squares, 10" x 10"

From the cream print, cut:
12 squares, 10½" x 10½"

From the lavender print, cut:
10 strips, 1½" wide; crosscut 6 strips into 17 segments, 10½" long

From the lime green print, cut:
10 squares, 1½" x 1½"
4 squares, 6" x 6"

From the large-scale purple print, cut:
6 strips, 6" wide

MAKING THE BLOCKS

1. Stack two striped 10" squares right side up with the stripes going in the same direction. Cut the squares in half horizontally and vertically to yield eight 5" squares. Repeat with the remaining 10 squares. Make two stacks of 24 squares *each*, with the stripes running in the same direction in each stack.

2. Place one stack of 5" squares next to your sewing machine with the stripes running horizontally. Place the remaining stack of squares next to them with the stripes running vertically. Sew a square from each stack together. The stripes should run perpendicular to each other. Repeat to make a total of 24 pairs. Press all seam allowances in the same direction.

Make 24.

3. Sew two pairs of squares together as shown, matching the center seams and edges to make a four-patch unit. Repeat to make a total of 12 units. Press the seam allowances in either direction.

Make 12.

4. Refer to "Working with Circles" on page 16 to determine your preferred appliqué method, and then cut out the circle appliqués from the four-patch units. *For fusible appliqué*, set the compass or circle cutter at 4" and cut an 8"-diameter circle from each unit, placing the point of the tool in the center of the unit where the seams intersect. *For freezer-paper appliqué*, use the same compass/circle cutter settings as for fusible appliqué to make 8"-diameter circle templates from freezer paper. Center a freezer-paper template on each pieced unit, and

then use a rotary cutter, scissors, or circle cutter to cut out the fabric circles ⅜" larger than the freezer-paper circles.

5. Using the appliqué method you selected in step 4, appliqué a circle to the center of a cream square so that the seams run horizontally and vertically. Repeat to make a total of six blocks. Center the remaining circles on the remaining cream squares with the seams running diagonally and appliqué them in place.

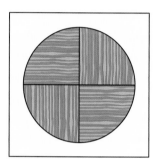

Make 6.

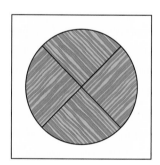

Make 6.

ASSEMBLING THE QUILT TOP

1. Refer to the quilt assembly diagram on page 37 to arrange the blocks into four horizontal rows of three blocks each, inserting a lavender 1½" x 10½" sashing segment between the blocks in each row.

2. Sew the blocks and sashing segments in each row together. Press the seam allowances toward the sashing.

3. To make the sashing rows, alternately sew three sashing segments and two lime green 1½" squares together. Press the seam allowances toward the sashing.

4. With seams matching, sew the block rows and sashing rows together, inserting a sashing row between block rows. Press the seam allowances toward the sashing rows.

5. Carefully square up the quilt top. Use a square ruler for the corners and a long ruler and rotary cutter for the sides.

ADDING THE BORDERS

For general instructions on measuring and sewing borders, refer to "Adding Borders" on page 91.

1. Measure the length and width of the quilt top and make a note of the measurements.

2. Trim two of the remaining lavender strips to the width measured, and sew the strips to the top and bottom of the quilt top. Press the seam allowances toward the border strips.

3. Sew the pieces you trimmed from the top and bottom border strips to one end of each of the remaining lavender strips. Trim these pieced strips to the length measured in step 1. Add a lime green 1½" square to the ends of each strip. Press the seam allowances toward the border strips. Sew the strips to the sides of the quilt top, matching the seams of the cornerstones. Press the seam allowances toward the border strips.

4. Measure the length and width of your quilt again, and make a note of the measurements.

5. Repeat step 2 to add the purple print top and bottom outer borders to the quilt top. Press the seam allowances toward the outer border strips.

6. Sew two of the remaining purple print strips together end to end, matching the pattern if necessary. Repeat to make one additional pieced strip. Trim the pieced strips to the length measured in step 4. Add a lime green 6" square to the ends of each strip. Press the seam allowances toward the border strips. Sew the strips to the sides of the quilt

top, matching the seams of the cornerstones. Press the seam allowances toward the border strips. Give yourself a pat on the back—your quilt top is done!

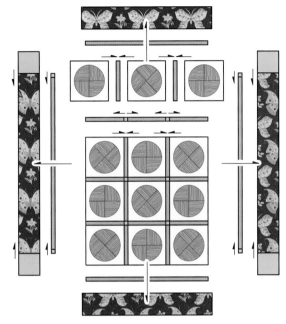

Quilt assembly

FINISHING THE QUILT

Referring to "Basic Quiltmaking Techniques," beginning on page 90, layer the quilt top with batting and backing fabric, and baste the layers together. Quilt as desired or choose a quilting design from "Quilting Ideas" on page 81. I used the smaller version of the loops and butterflies design (shown on page 88) for the quilting on the backgrounds of the blocks and the larger variation of the same design for the wide borders. Bind the edges with the striped 2"-wide binding strips.

CIRCLES IN THE ATTIC

This wall hanging uses regular stripes printed parallel to the selvage. Beginners may want to choose solid or print background fabrics for easier piecing. This wall hanging uses a Free Spirit striped fabric designed by Michael James. It's a regular stripe that is printed parallel to the selvage.

By Leigh E. McDonald, 2005

Skill Level: All
Finished Quilt Size: 45" x 45"
Finished Block Size: 11⅛" x 11⅛"

MATERIALS

All yardages are based on 42"-wide fabric.

1⅓ yards of light-value stripe, print, or solid for block backgrounds

1⅓ yards of dark-value stripe or solid for sashing, outer border, and binding

⅝ yard *each* of two different medium- to dark-value stripes or prints for circle appliqués

1 fat quarter *each* of two different medium-value stripes or prints for circle appliqués

⅜ yard of medium-value stripe or solid for sashing

3⅛ yards of fabric for backing (pieced lengthwise or crosswise)

51" x 51" piece of batting

CUTTING

All measurements include ¼"-wide seam allowances. Cut all strips across the width of the fabric.

From the light-value stripe, print, or solid, cut:
16 squares, 10" x 10"

From the dark-value stripe or solid, cut:
12 strips, 2½" wide; crosscut into 24 segments, 14" long
5 strips, 2" wide

From the medium-value stripe or solid, cut:
4 strips, 2½" wide; crosscut into 8 segments, 14" long

MAKING THE BLOCKS

1. Refer to "Working with Circles" on page 16 to determine your preferred appliqué method, and then cut out the circle appliqués from the medium- and dark-value fabrics. *For fusible appliqué*, set the compass or circle cutter at 3¾" and make two 7½"-diameter circles from *each* of the medium-value stripe or print fat quarters (4 total), and six 7½"-diameter circles from *each* of the two different medium- to dark-value stripes or prints (12 total). *For freezer-paper appliqué*, use the same compass/circle cutter setting as for fusible appliqué to make 16 circle templates from freezer paper. Press two onto each of the medium-value stripe or print fat quarters and six onto each of the two different medium- to dark-value stripes or prints, and then use a rotary cutter, scissors, or circle cutter to cut out the fabric circles ⅜" larger than the freezer-paper circles.

2. Using the appliqué method you selected in step 1, appliqué each circle to a light-value 10" square, centering the circle on the square so that the stripes of the circle make a diagonal line from corner to corner. Make sure all the background stripes run vertically when you position the circles.

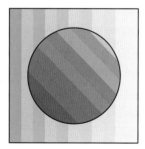

3. Set aside the four squares with medium-value circles for the center of the quilt top. Divide the remaining appliquéd squares into two equal piles. Arrange the squares in one pile so that background stripes are running vertically. Arrange the squares in the remaining pile so that the background strips are running horizontally. Cut the squares in each pile in half diagonally from corner to corner as shown. Label the triangles in one pile A and in the other pile B.

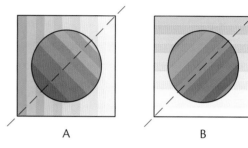

A　　　　　　　　　B

4. Take the stacks of triangles to your sewing machine, keeping the A and B triangles separate. Sew a dark-value stripe or solid 14"-long sashing segment to the left edge of each A triangle, matching the triangle and segment at the top edge of the triangle and backstitching ¼" from the bottom corner. Trim the excess sashing even with the diagonal edge of each triangle. Before you cut, place the outside edge of the sashing segment on one of the lines on your cutting mat and make sure it lies straight. Press the seam allowance toward the sashing segment. Sew a dark-value sashing segment to the bottom edge of each B triangle in the same manner; trim the excess sashing even with the diagonal edge.

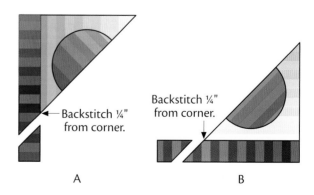

Backstitch ¼" from corner.

Backstitch ¼" from corner.

A　　　　　　　　　B

What's on Top?

When sewing the sashing segments to the A triangles, place the sashing on the bottom, nearest the sewing machine, and the triangle on top. When sewing the B triangles, place the triangle on the bottom and the sashing on the top.

5. Pin each A triangle to a B triangle along the long diagonal edges, matching the edges of the circles and the sashing. If you used a striped background fabric, try to match up the stripes the best you can. Sometimes it works, sometimes it doesn't. Sew the triangles together, being careful not to stretch bias edges. Press the seam allowance to one side. Make 12 blocks.

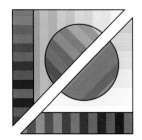 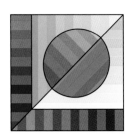

Make 12.

6. Repeat steps 3–5 with the four squares with medium-value circles that you set aside earlier and the medium-value sashing segments. Make four additional blocks.

ASSEMBLING THE QUILT TOP

1. Refer to the quilt assembly diagram at right to arrange the blocks into four horizontal rows of four blocks each, placing the four blocks with medium-value circles in the center of the arrangement. Make sure the sashing segments are positioned as shown. Move the blocks around, keeping the medium-value blocks in the center, until you are pleased with the overall appearance of your quilt.

2. Sew the blocks in each row together, matching the edges, sashing seams, and the center seams of the medium-value blocks. Press the seam allowances in opposite directions from row to row.

3. Sew the rows together, matching edges and seams. Press the seam allowances in one direction.

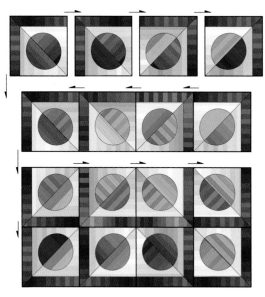

Quilt assembly

FINISHING THE QUILT

Referring to "Basic Quiltmaking Technniques," beginning on page 90, layer the quilt top with batting and backing fabric, and baste the layers together. Quilt as desired. I echo quilted around the circles. You could also quilt along the diagonal lines if you used a striped fabric, or add diagonal lines to the background of each block if you used a print or solid fabric. See "Quilting Ideas" on page 81 for more quilting designs and suggestions. Bind the edges with the 2"-wide dark-value stripe or solid strips.

BALLS IN THE AIR

Arranged on a dark background, the circles in this quilt appear to float in space. Additional interest is created within some of the appliqués through curved cutting and piecing that brings two or three fabrics together.

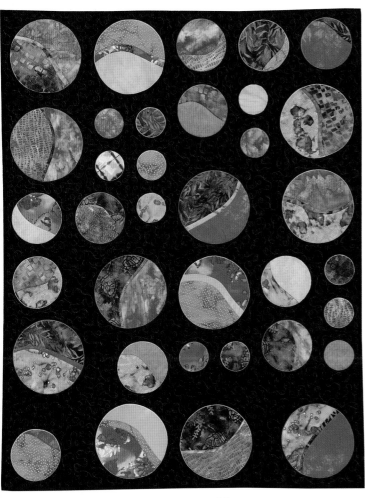

By Leigh E. McDonald, 2005

Skill Level: Intermediate/Advanced
Finished Quilt Size: 38½" x 49½"
Finished Block Sizes: 9" x 9", 6½" x 6½", and 4½" x 4½"

MATERIALS

All yardages are based on 42"-wide fabric.

12 fat quarters of assorted bright hand-dyed or batik fabrics

2⅝ yards of black print for background and binding

2⅞ yards of fabric for backing* (pieced crosswise)

45" x 56" piece of batting

*If the backing fabric is wide enough after prewashing to suit your own personal requirements, you may need only one length. In that case, purchase 1¾ yards.

CUTTING

Before you begin cutting, refer to "Working with Circles" on page 16 to determine your preferred appliqué method. If you decide to use the fusible-web method, take the fusible-web test on page 44 first to make sure the web is compatible with your machine. If it is, apply the fusible web to the wrong side of the bright fat quarters before you cut out any pieces. Remove the paper backing before sewing.

All measurements include ¼"-wide seam allowances. Cut all strips across the width of the fabric.

From the black print, cut:
12 squares, 9½" x 9½"
11 squares, 7" x 7"
12 squares, 5" x 5"
1 rectangle, 3" x 9½"
4 rectangles, 3" x 7"
1 strip, 2½" x 20½"
2 rectangles, 2½" x 9½"
1 rectangle, 2½" x 5"
3 rectangles, 1" x 7"
5 strips, 2" wide

From *each* of the 12 fat quarters, cut:

1 square, 9" x 9" (12 total)

1 square, 7" x 7" (12 total; 1 will not be used)

1 square, 5" x 5" (12 total)

Fusible-Web Test

Apply a piece of fusible-web to the wrong side of a scrap of fabric and remove the paper backing. With the right side up, sew a line through the fused fabric. If the web sticks to the sewing machine and doesn't move freely, then use the freezer-paper appliqué method for this quilt. Sticking might occur if the base of your sewing machine is metal.

MAKING THE BLOCKS

You will be making three circle appliqués from each stack of fabrics. For a subtle look, pick three different types of prints that have the same value. For instance, use three medium-value fabrics. For a more visually divided circle in which the curved stripe in the center shows up clearly, pick three different values or types of prints. For instance, layer a geometric, a polka-dot, and a floral square together.

1. Pick three bright 9" squares that you like together and stack them right sides up with the edges aligned. Using a small rotary cutter, cut two gentle curves, parallel to each other and 1" to 2" apart, through the approximate center of the layers. This will cut each square into three pieces.

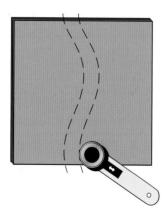

2. Remove the top two layers from the right-hand side and place them on the bottom of the right-hand stack, right sides up. Take the top layer from the middle section and place it on the bottom of the middle stack, right side up.

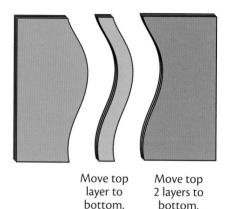

Move top layer to bottom.   Move top 2 layers to bottom.

3. Refer to "Cutting and Sewing Curves" on page 47 to sew the three pieces on the top of the stack together, being careful to pick up only the top layer if you are using the fusible-web method; fusible web tends to make the pieces stick together. Do not worry about the edges lining up, because they will be cut off when you cut out the circles later. Sew the next two layers together in the same manner to make a total of three pieced squares. Press the seam allowances in one direction, whichever leaves the piece flattest. (*Do not press with an iron if you're using the fusible-web method; finger-press only!*)

4. Repeat steps 1–3 until all the 9" squares have been cut apart and sewn back together. All of the curves do not have to be directly in the center or exactly alike, but the narrow piece should be close to the center.

5. *For fusible appliqué,* set the compass or circle cutter at 3½" and make a 7"-diameter circle from each pieced square. *For freezer-paper appliqué,* use the same compass/circle cutter setting as for fusible appliqué to make 12 circle templates from freezer paper. Press the templates onto the center of the pieced squares, and then use a rotary cutter, scissors, or circle cutter to cut out the fabric circles ⅜" larger than the freezer-paper circles.

6. Pick three bright 7" squares that you like together and stack them right sides up with the edges aligned. Cut a gentle curve through the layers to divide them in half. The cut can be anywhere on the square, but don't make it too close to the edges.

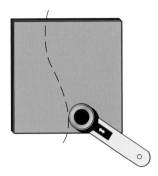

7. Remove the top layer from the right-hand side and place it on the bottom of the right-hand stack, right side up. Sew the pieces from each layer together as before. Press the seam allowances to one side. (Remember to finger-press if you're using the fusible-web method.) Clip the curves of the seam allowance to make it lie flatter and trim the seam allowances to reduce bulk. There will be one square that you do not use; set it aside for another project.

8. *For fusible appliqué,* set the compass or circle cutter at 2½" and make a 5"-diameter circle from each pieced square from step 7. *For freezer-paper appliqué,* use the same compass/circle cutter setting as for fusible appliqué to make 11 circle templates from freezer paper. Press the templates onto the center of the pieced squares, and then use a rotary cutter, scissors, or circle cutter to cut out the fabric circles ⅜" larger than the freezer-paper circles.

9. *For fusible appliqué,* set the compass or circle cutter at 1½" and make a 3"-diameter circle from each bright 5" square. *For freezer-paper appliqué,* use the same compass/circle cutter setting as for fusible appliqué to make 12 circle templates from freezer paper. Press the templates onto the center of the pieced squares, and then use a rotary cutter, scissors, or circle cutter to cut out the fabric circles ⅜" larger than the freezer-paper circles.

10. Using the appliqué method you selected earlier, appliqué a 7"-diameter pieced circle to each black 9½" square. Appliqué a 5" pieced circle to each black 7" square, and a 3" circle to each black 5" square.

Fusing Pieced Circles
Place the point of the iron at the center of the circle, making sure that the seams lie flat in one direction. Press from the center of the circle outward, flattening as you go. Ease the excess with your fingers, making sure not to press in a pleat. Steam press when finished.

ASSEMBLING THE QUILT TOP

1. Arrange and sew together the blocks, the black rectangles, and the black 2½" x 20½" strip into sections A–G as shown. Vary the placement of the appliquéd circles in each section to make sure the colors are sprinkled around the quilt top. Press the seam allowances in the directions indicated.

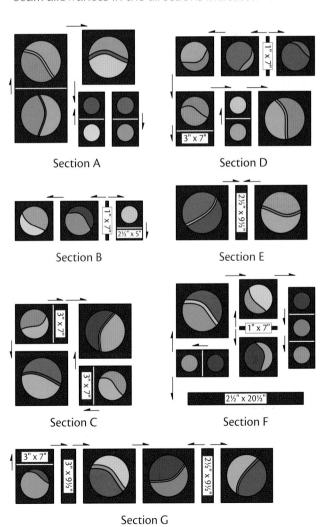

2. Refer to the assembly diagram below to sew sections A–F together before adding section G. Press the seam allowances in the directions indicated.

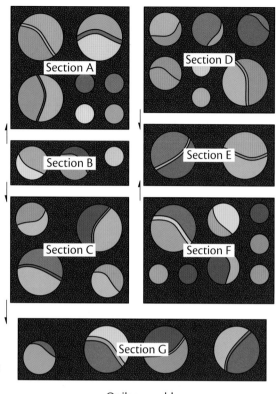

Quilt assembly

FINISHING THE QUILT

Referring to "Basic Quiltmaking Techniques," beginning on page 90, layer the quilt top with batting and backing fabric, and baste the layers together. Quilt as desired. I used the classic loop design (shown on page 85) for this quilt. See "Quilting Ideas" on page 81 for more quilting designs and suggestions. Bind the edges with the black 2"-wide strips.

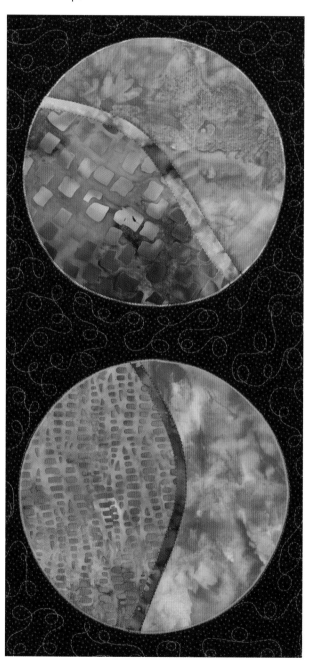

Cutting and Sewing Curves

The key to sewing a nice curve is in the cutting. The curve should be gentle enough that you see it as a curve but not so tight that it will be difficult to sew.

Pin the curved pieces together at the deepest part of the curve first and then work the fabric from that point to the outside edges, matching the edges of the fabrics and pinning as you go. It's not important to match up the outside edges of the pieces because you're going to cut them off anyway, but the edges at the deepest point of the curve should match. When pinning a curve, catch the tiniest amount of each fabric at the ¼" seam line only. The fabric must be able to move as you manipulate it under the sewing-machine needle. You will use more pins on a deep curve than on a gentle curve. The best pins to use when sewing curves are very fine silk pins, because they take up less space in the fabric and can catch a tiny bite of fabric and hold it.

There are two sides of a curve: the convex, or mountain, side and the concave, or valley, side. Place the convex side of the curve against the sewing-machine base and the concave side of the curve on top. Sew the seam, using a stitch length of about 14 stitches per inch. Take out the pins before you get to them and whenever you need to release the fabric so that you don't sew a pucker into the seam. *Sew slowly.* This is not a time when faster is better. When you first start sewing curves you will not be able to manipulate the fabric fast enough, even when sewing slowly.

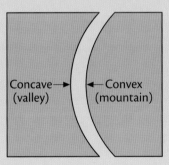

Concave→ (valley)   ←Convex (mountain)

Sometimes you may need to sew an S-shaped curve. The easiest way to do this is to pin the first curve and start sewing from the center of the curve. Just as before, you have the convex, or mountain, side of the curve down against the machine. Sew toward the outside edge. Take the fabric out of the sewing machine, pin the second curve, and then flip the fabric over and begin sewing at the point where you started before, overlapping a couple of stitches. Going in the opposite direction, sew toward the outside edge. Doing it this way allows you to have the convex side down, making it easier to sew the seam.

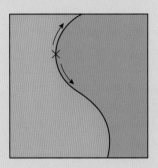

S-curve.
Sew from X in direction of arrows.

I move my hands differently when sewing curves. Often I will insert a finger between the two layers of fabric to guide one layer along so that it matches the edge of the other. Keep a loose hold on the fabrics rather than a tight hold. A big key is to only worry about matching the edges ¼" in front of the needle at a time. Because the fabric cups and is not flat when you are sewing a curve, it won't work if you try to match the entire seam.

Press the seam allowance in the direction it wants to go. If the curve doesn't lie flat once it's sewn and ironed, then clip the seam allowance perpendicular to the seam line without cutting the stitching. This releases tension on the seam and allows the curve to lie flat.

HARVEST MOON

Reminiscent of a Japanese screen, this long, narrow wall hanging literally shines. The metallic thread used in the quilting contributes to the glow. I recommend the fusible-web appliqué method for this quilt and the instructions have been written accordingly.

By Leigh E. McDonald, 2005

Skill Level: Intermediate/Advanced
Finished Quilt Size: 31¼" x 56¼"
Finished Block Sizes: 4½" x 9½", 4½" x 4½"

MATERIALS

All yardages are based on 42"-wide fabric.

1½ yards of brown batik for background

1¼ yards *total* of assorted hand-dyed or batik solids for appliqués

1 yard of black batik for sashing and binding

2 yards of fabric for backing

38" x 63" piece of batting

2½ yards of paper-backed fusible transfer web

CUTTING

All measurements include ¼"-wide seam allowances. Cut all strips across the width of the fabric.

From the brown batik, cut:
9 strips, 5" wide; crosscut into:
- 30 rectangles, 5" x 10"
- 6 squares, 5" x 5"

From the black batik, cut:
11 strips, 1¼" wide; crosscut 4 strips into 30 segments, 1¼" x 5"
5 strips, 2" wide

CUTTING OUT THE CIRCLES AND DOUGHNUTS

1. Apply fusible web to the wrong side of each of the assorted hand-dyed and batik solids.

2. Refer to "Working with Circles" on page 16 to cut out the circles and doughnuts from the fused fabrics as follows:

a. Set the compass or circle cutter at 2½" and make 22 circles with a 5" diameter. Reset the compass/circle cutter at 1⅛". From 18 of the 5" circles, cut a 2¼" circle to create a doughnut. The circles from the center of the doughnut will not be used but can be saved for future quilt projects.

b. Set the compass/circle cutter at 2" and make 14 circles with a 4" diameter. Reset the compass/circle cutter at 1⅛" and make a 2¼" circle to create a doughnut. The circles from the center of the doughnut will not be used.

c. Set the compass/circle cutter at 1½" and cut out 11 circles with a 3" diameter.

3. Remove the paper backing from the circles and doughnuts. Gently fold the pieces in half and finger-press the folds. Lay your ruler on the pressed line and cut each piece in half with your rotary cutter.

MAKING THE BLOCKS

1. Stack a 4" half doughnut on a 5" half doughnut, right sides up, and fuse them together, using a Teflon pressing sheet under the pieces. Let the pieces cool and then peel the double-doughnut piece off of the pressing sheet. Repeat this process with all but 8 to 10 of the remaining half-doughnut pieces. Mix up the colors for more variety.

2. Arrange the double and single half doughnuts and the half circles on the brown batik rectangles and squares as desired, using the placement diagrams at right as a guide only. There are many ways the pieces can be arranged. Just be sure the

straight edges of the fused pieces are aligned with the long straight edges of the background pieces, and make sure to mix up the colors. Fuse the pieces in place and then stitch along the curved edges, using either monofilament or a decorative thread. Refer to "Embellishing Tools, Tips, and Techniques" on page 21 for creative tips and ideas for embellishing the appliqué edges.

ASSEMBLING THE QUILT TOP

1. Refer to the assembly diagram at right and use a design wall to arrange the blocks and black batik 1¼" x 5" horizontal sashing strips into six vertical rows. The appliqué placement will be slightly different for your quilt, but each row should consist of five

rectangle blocks and one square block. Once again, mix up the colors around the quilt.

2. Sew the blocks and sashing strips in each row together. Press the seam allowances toward the sashing.

3. Piece the remaining black batik 1¼"-wide strips together to make five 56¼"-long vertical sashing strips. Sew the rows together, inserting a sashing strip between each row. Press the seam allowances toward the sashing.

FINISHING THE QUILT

Referring to "Basic Quiltmaking Techniques," beginning on page 90, layer the quilt top with batting and backing fabric, and baste the layers together. Quilt as desired. I used a combination of stitching in the ditch and a tiny classic stipple for my version of this quilt. See "Quilting Ideas" on page 81 for more quilting designs and suggestions. Bind the edges with the black batik 2"-wide strips.

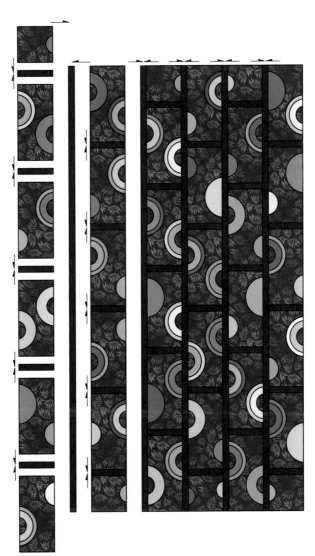

Quilt assembly

CARNIVAL

Like the spinning lights on the Ferris wheel at the carnival, this quilt lights up the wall with color and pattern. Use the fusible-web appliqué method for quick and easy results.

By Leigh E. McDonald, 2007

Skill Level: Intermediate

Finished Quilt Size: 45½" x 45½"

Finished Block Size: 16¾" x 16¾"

MATERIALS

All yardages are based on 42"-wide fabric.

1 yard of black-with-rainbow spiral print for pieced border and binding

⅞ yard of white-with-black dot print for block backgrounds and pieced border cornerstones

⅞ yard of black-with-white circle print for block backgrounds and pieced border cornerstones

⅓ yard of dark blue violet print for pieced border

1 fat quarter *each* of two different red prints for appliqués

1 fat quarter *each* of two different yellow gold prints for appliqués

1 fat quarter *each* of two different lime green prints for appliqués

1 fat quarter *each* of two different blue green prints for appliqués

Scraps of two different orange prints for appliqués

Scraps of two different red violet prints for appliqués

Scraps of two different blue prints for appliqués

Scraps of two different blue violet prints for appliqués

3 yards of fabric for backing (pieced in either direction)

5 yards of paper-backed fusible web

3 yards of tear-away stabilizer (optional, but recommended)

2 yards of lightweight fusible interfacing (optional, see "Interfacing Interceder" on page 54)

51" x 51" piece of batting

Interfacing Interceder

The background fabrics may shadow through lighter-colored fabric, such as the yellow gold prints or the lime green print. Test to see if background fabric will show through by placing the background fabric right side up behind one layer of the lighter print. If you can see the background print, fuse lightweight interfacing to the wrong side of your light-value fabrics before applying the fusible web or cutting out the pieces. The added layer will reduce or eliminate the visibility of the background color.

CUTTING

All measurements include ¼"-wide seam allowances. Cut all strips across the width of the fabric.

From the white-with-black dot print, cut:
2 squares, 18½" x 18½"
2 squares, 7" x 7"

From the black-with-white circle print, cut:
2 squares, 18½" x 18½"
2 squares, 7" x 7"

From the black-with-rainbow spiral print, cut:
4 strips, 4¾" x 33"
5 strips, 2" wide

From the dark blue violet print, cut:
4 strips, 2" x 33"

CUTTING OUT THE CIRCLES AND DOUGHNUTS

1. You will be making two A units and two B units from the circles and doughnuts. Each unit will have a warm-color version (reds and yellows) and a cool-color version (blues and greens) for a total of four units. The A units will be combined later to make the A blocks. The same is true for the B units. Group your background and appliqué fabrics together for each unit before applying the fusible web and cutting out the circles and doughnuts. This enables you to see whether they go together well and helps keep you organized through the cutting process. The diagram above right shows the placement of the doughnuts and circles on the background squares. The numbers indicate the outer dimensions of the pieces.

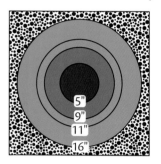 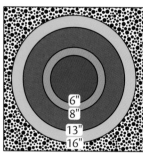

Unit A   Unit B

Make 1 A unit and 1 B unit with cool-color appliqués on black-with-white background.

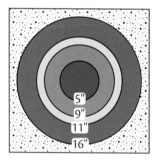 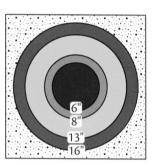

Unit A   Unit B

Make 1 A unit and 1 B unit with warm-color appliqués on white-with-black background.

2. Apply fusible web to the wrong side of each of the appliqué fabrics.

3. Refer to "Working with Circles" on page 16 to cut out the circles and doughnuts from the fused fabrics as follows. You will not use the inner circles from the doughnuts. Set them aside for another project.

   a. Set the yardstick compass at 8". From *each* of the red prints and the lime green prints, make a 16"-diameter circle. Reset the yardstick compass at 6¼". From one red circle and one lime circle, cut out a 12½"-diameter circle to create a doughnut. Reset the yardstick compass at 5¼". From the remaining red and lime circle, cut out a 10½"-diameter circle to create a doughnut.

   b. Set the yardstick compass at 6½". From one of the yellow gold prints and one of the blue green prints, make a 13"-diameter circle. Reset the yardstick compass or a circle cutter at 3¾" and cut out a 7½" diameter circle from each circle to create a doughnut.

c. Set the yardstick compass at 5½". From the other yellow gold print and the other blue green print, make an 11"-diameter circle. Reset the yardstick compass or a circle cutter at 4¼" and cut out an 8½"-diameter circle from each circle to create a doughnut.

d. Set the yardstick compass at 4½". From one orange print and one blue print, make a 9"-diameter circle. Set the yardstick compass or a regular compass or circle cutter at 2¼" and cut out a 4½"-diameter circle from each circle to create a doughnut.

e. Set the yardstick compass or circle cutter at 4". From the other orange print and the other blue print, make an 8"-diameter circle. Set the yardstick compass or a regular compass or circle cutter at 2¾" and cut out a 5½"-diameter circle from each circle to create a doughnut.

f. Set the regular compass or circle cutter at 3". From one red violet print and one blue violet print, make a 6"-diameter circle.

g. Set the regular compass or circle cutter at 2½". From the other red violet print and the other blue violet print, make a 5"-diameter circle.

h. Set the regular compass or circle cutter at 2". From the remainder of one red print, one orange print, one lime green print, and one blue print, make a 4"-diameter circle.

4. Remove the paper backing from each piece.

MAKING THE BLOCKS

1. Set aside the red, orange, lime green, and blue 4" circles for the border cornerstones. Referring to "Working with Circles" on page 16, use the diagram from step 1 of "Cutting Out the Circles and Doughnuts" to center and fuse the remaining circles and doughnuts to the 18½" background squares.

2. Stitch along the curved edges, using either monofilament or a decorative thread. Refer to "Embellishing Tools, Tips, and Techniques" on page 21 for creative tips and ideas for embellishing the appliqué edges.

Consistency Counts

For interest, you can vary the width of the satin stitch from one circle edge to another within the A units, but you must duplicate the stitch widths and locations for the second A block. The same goes for the B blocks. The easiest way to do this without getting confused is to keep the first block of each kind right next to the sewing machine when you are working on the second block of the same kind. Refer to it every time you change thread color or stitch width. The color of the thread does not have to match, just the width of the stitch.

3. Stack the two A blocks right sides up on the cutting mat, matching the raw edges and placing the lower-left corners of the blocks at the 0 mark on the mat.

4. With a 6" x 24" ruler and your rotary cutter, cut the two blocks in half horizontally and vertically at the 9¼" marks on the cutting mat. Move the four squares apart on the cutting mat, being careful not to shift the two layers. Carefully cut each 9¼" square in half diagonally, corner to corner, making sure you are cutting through the center small circle to the outside corner. Think of cutting a pie. Move the stacks back together.

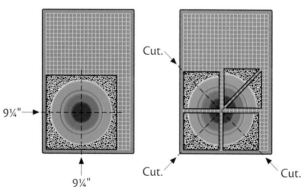

5. Starting at the upper-right corner of the divided pieces, put the top layer of every other stack on the bottom of the stack, right side up. This will alternate the background prints.

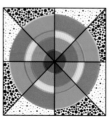

6. Working with the triangles from the top layer, sew the two half-square triangles in each corner together to make four squares. Pin the seams, matching the stitching lines around the outside of the appliqués, to help keep the pieces from shifting when sewing. Sew from the outside edge toward the center. Press the seam allowances to one side, all in the same direction.

Sewing Tip for Triangles

When sewing the pieces together, increase the sewing machine's stitch length to 12 stitches per inch and sew *slowly* over the satin-stitched lines. Be careful not to stretch the bias edges when sewing the triangles, especially on the nonfused background fabrics.

7. Sew the upper-left square to the lower-left square. Clip the triangle points in the seam allowance and press the seam open. Sew the upper-right square to the lower-right square in the same manner.

8. Pin and sew the two halves together slowly to make a block, matching the stitched lines and the center points. You may have to sew up to the center point from each outside edge and backstitch. It will be extremely bulky at the center point. Press the seam allowance open.

9. Repeat steps 6–8 with the triangles on the bottom layer to make an additional A block (two total).

Hot Stuff

Press from the back whenever possible and be careful not to melt your metallic or rayon/polyester threads with the iron. Keep the temperature of the iron set on polyester, rather than cotton.

10. Repeat steps 3–9 with the B units to make two B blocks.

ASSEMBLING THE QUILT TOP

1. Refer to the assembly diagram on page 57 to arrange the blocks in two vertical rows of two blocks each, with one A block and one B block in each row.

2. Sew the blocks in each row together. Press the seam allowances in opposite directions. Trim the ends of the triangles in the seam allowances after you make sure your points match.

3. Sew the rows together, matching seams. Press the seam allowance to one side. The center of your quilt is complete!

You're Not Crazy, It May Be Wavy

At this point your quilt top may buckle a little bit. This is because of the difference in the fabric weights between the single layer of fabric in the background of the blocks and the multiple layers created by the appliqués. The glue from the fusible web also adds stiffness to the circles. The buckling will get better when the borders are added.

ADDING THE BORDERS

1. To make the cornerstone blocks, center a red 4"-diameter circle on one white-with-black dot print 7" square and an orange 4"-diameter circle on the remaining white-with-black dot print 7" square; fuse the circles in place. Repeat with the lime green and blue 4"-diameter circles and the black-with-white circle print 7" squares. Stitch around the edges of the circles, using the same thread and stitch that you used for the blocks in the quilt center.

2. Stack a warm-color appliqué square on top of a cool-color appliqué square. With your rotary cutter and ruler, cut the squares in half diagonally from corner to corner in both directions. Cut slowly and make sure the pieces do not move when you are cutting them. This will divide the layers into four stacks.

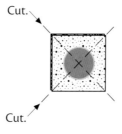

3. Move the top layer of every other stack to the bottom, right side up. This will alternate the background prints.

4. Working with the triangles from the top layer, sew two adjacent triangles together to make a pieced triangle, matching the stitching lines around the outside edges of the appliqués. Repeat with the remaining two triangles. Press the seam allowances in the same direction. Sew the pieced triangles together, again matching the stitching line and center seams. Press the seam allowance to one side to complete the block.

5. Repeat step 4 with the triangles on the bottom layer to make one additional cornerstone block.

6. Repeat steps 2–5 with the remaining two appliquéd squares to make two additional cornerstone blocks (four total).

7. Sew a dark blue violet strip to a spiral print 4¾" x 33" strip along the long edges. Press the seam allowance toward the spiral print strips. Repeat to make a total of four border strips.

8. Sew a border strip to the sides of the quilt top, placing the blue violet strip toward the quilt center. Press the seam allowances toward the border strips.

Easing the Difference

If the length of your quilt top isn't quite the same as the border strips, pin the pieces together, matching the ends and centers, and then place the piece with the excess fabric on the bottom. The feed dogs will help ease in the extra fabric.

9. Refer to the assembly diagram to sew a cornerstone block to each end of the two remaining border strips. Pay close attention to the position of the blue violet strip and the colors and positions of the cornerstone blocks. Press the seam allowances away from the cornerstone blocks.

10. Sew the top and bottom borders to the quilt top, matching the cornerstone corners with the quilt-top corners. Press the seam allowances toward the borders.

Quilt assembly

FINISHING THE QUILT

Referring to "Basic Quiltmaking Techniques," beginning on page 90, layer the quilt top with batting and backing fabric, and baste the layers together. Quilt next to the lines of stitching around the appliqués, but stay away from the centers where it is bulky. You can quilt on one side of the stitching line or on both sides. I recommend using a stipple quilting design on the background of the quilt top. This will help ease out any waffling in the quilt top. See "Quilting Ideas" on page 81 for stipple quilting designs. This quilt is an excellent candidate for the addition of beading elements. For ideas on choices of beads and beading techniques see "Embellishing Tools, Tips, and Techniques" on page 21. Bind the quilt with the black-with-rainbow spiral print 2"-wide strips.

CLOCKWORKS

The colors of the fabrics used in the background of this wall hanging remind me of a sunset, but the look could easily change to a night sky if you selected lots of navy and violet prints. I used approximately 30 different fabrics for the background blocks of this quilt to heighten the visual interest. Leftover fused fabrics from other projects are perfect for the gear appliqués in this quilt.

By Leigh E. McDonald, 2007

Skill Level: Advanced
Finished Quilt Size: 54½" x 54½"
Finished Block Size: 18" x 18"

MATERIALS

All yardages are based on 42"-wide fabric.

1¼ yards *total* of assorted medium- to dark-value red, orange, and blue green fat quarters or scraps for background

1⅛ yards *total* of assorted dark-value navy, violet, blue green, and burgundy fat quarters or scraps for background

1⅛ yards *total* of assorted light- to medium-value blue, blue green, pink, and peach fat quarters or scraps for background

1 yard of light-value solid for clock appliqués

¾ yard *total* of assorted bright hand-dyed solids for gear appliqués

Scraps of medium-value solid for clock face center-circle appliqué

½ yard of medium- to dark-value print for binding

3½ yards of fabric for backing (pieced lengthwise)

61" x 61" piece of batting

2 yards of tear-away stabilizer (optional)

1½ yards of paper-backed fusible transfer web

Freezer paper

Template plastic

CUTTING

All measurements include ¼"-wide seam allowances. Cut all strips across the width of the fabric.

From the assorted light- to medium-value fat quarters or scraps, cut a *total* of:
32 rectangles, 2¾" x 5"
64 squares, 2¾" x 2¾"
4 squares, 9½" x 9½"*

From the assorted medium- to dark-value fat quarters or scraps, cut a *total* of:
16 rectangles, 2¾" x 5"
32 squares, 2¾" x 2¾"
8 squares, 9½" x 9½"*

From the assorted dark-value fat quarters or scraps, cut a *total* of:
32 rectangles, 2¾" x 5"
64 squares, 2¾" x 2¾"
4 squares, 9½" x 9½"*

From the binding fabric, cut:
6 strips, 2" wide

Cut each square from a different fabric.

MAKING THE BACKGROUND BLOCKS

1. Using the light- to medium-value rectangles and 2¾" squares, sew two squares and one rectangle together as shown to make a pieced block unit. Make 32. I recommend using pieces from the same color family to make each unit, occasionally adding a piece from another color family. Press the seam allowances in the directions shown.

2. Repeat step 1 with the medium- to- dark-value rectangles and 2¾" squares to make 16 units, and with the dark-value rectangles and 2¾" squares to make 32 units.

3. In the upper-left corner of your design wall, arrange 16 light- to medium-value units into four horizontal rows of four units each. You can rotate these units any way you like. A sample arrangement

is shown below. Try to arrange the colors so that one flows into another.

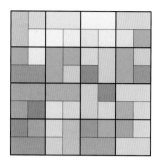

Sample arrangement

4. Next to the step 3 arrangement, lay out the four light- to medium-value 9½" squares in two horizontal rows of two squares each, trying to maintain the flow of color. Arrange the remaining 16 block units next to these squares as you did in step 3 to complete the layout of the first row.

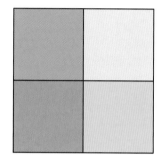

5. For the second row, use the medium- to dark-value pieces. Begin with four 9½" squares, arranged in two rows of two squares each, then the 16 pieced block units, followed by the remaining four 9½" squares.

6. The third row is made up of the dark-value pieces. Lay them out in the same manner as the first row.

Background Blending

Think of the background as a sunset or sunrise. I chose a sunset and put all my darks on the bottom and my light and medium blocks at the top. A sunrise would be the opposite, with all the light-value blocks on the bottom and the darks on the top. When you are placing the blocks on your design wall, don't worry about the arrangement of the blocks as much as the blending of the colors from one block to the next. Try to avoid hard lines where the color in one block is a different value or color from the block next to it. Twist and turn the block units and squares until you get a good blending of color.

7. When you are satisfied with the arrangement of the pieces, sew the pieces into blocks. You will make 16-unit blocks from the units you made in step 1 and Four Patch blocks from the 9½" squares. Work with the pieces one row at a time. To make the 16-unit blocks, separate the pieces as they are arranged into four rows of four units each. Sew the units in each row together. Press the seam allowances in opposite directions from row to row. Sew the rows together to complete the block. Press the seam allowances in one direction. Repeat this for all the units to make a total of five blocks. Press the seam allowances for all the 16-unit blocks in the same direction. Place the blocks back on the design wall as you finish them.

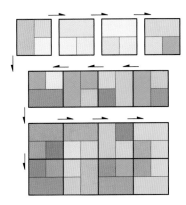

To make the Four Patch blocks, sew the squares in each row together. Press the seam allowances in opposite directions. Sew the rows together. Press the seam allowance in the opposite direction as the 16-unit blocks. Make a total of four blocks. Place the blocks back on the design wall as you finish them.

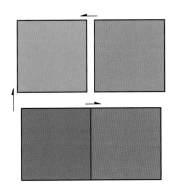

MAKING THE CLOCK BLOCKS

1. The clock faces were made using the freezer-paper method so that the background block fabrics wouldn't show through. Referring to "Working with Circles" on page 16, set the yardstick compass at 6¾" and make four 13½"-diameter circles from freezer paper. Using a regular compass or circle cutter set at ¾", make four 1½"-diameter circles from freezer paper. Press the large circle templates onto the light-value solid and the four small circles onto the medium-value solid, and then use a rotary cutter, scissors, or circle cutter to cut out the fabric circles ⅜" larger than the freezer-paper circles.

2. Appliqué a small circle to the center of each large circle.

3. Fold each circle into twelfths as shown.

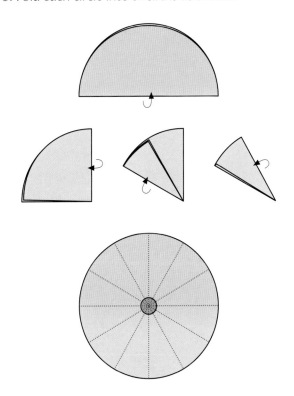

4. Using the fold lines, mark the placement of the clock hands and numerals with a water-soluble pen or other marking tool, remembering to allow for appliqué seam allowance. I marked the numeral placement ⅞" from the outer circle edges. The hand length was measured from the center circle, with the short hand on each clock 4" long and the long hand 5½" long. You can make the hands reflect any time that you want.

5. Stitch the clock details. There are several ways you can do this. If you have an embroidery machine, you can stitch the actual numbers on the face. Or you can use a satin stitch on your sewing machine and stitch one or two wide, solid lines at the position of each number on the clock. Stitch the hands of the clock with a solid satin-stitched line and then add arrow points by sewing toward that line at an angle, or going from a narrow zigzag to a wide zigzag as you reach the hand. You could also do the hands without the arrow points. I recommend using a piece of stabilizer under the clock fabric for any of these stitching methods.

 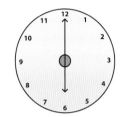

Fun Faces
Use your imagination to make the clock faces. None of them need be the same. Use different color threads or add beads and other embellishments. You can even use fabric paint to paint the details rather than stitching them.

6. Once your clock faces are completed, center and appliqué one to each of the Four Patch background blocks. Return the blocks to your design wall.

MAKING THE CLOCK GEARS

1. Apply fusible web to the wrong side of each of the assorted bright hand-dyed solids.

2. Refer to "Working with Circles" on page 16 to cut out the circles and doughnuts from the fused fabrics as follows:
   a. Set the compass or circle cutter at 2⅛" and make 20 circles with a 4¼" diameter.
   b. Set the compass or circle cutter at 1½" and make 17 circles with a 3" diameter. Reset the compass at ½" and cut out a 1"-diameter circle from each 3"-diameter circle to create a doughnut. Cut out 10 additional 1"-diameter circles.

3. Trace the gear template on page 63 onto template plastic and cut it out. Use the template to trace the shape onto 10 of the 4¼" circles, aligning the outer edges. You will fuse these shapes to the remaining 10 circles, so plan accordingly. Trace the center circle onto some but not all of the circles. Cut out the template shape. Remove the paper backing from the template shapes and the circles. Fuse one piece to each of the remaining 4¼" circles, using a Teflon pressing sheet under the pieces. For the gear shapes from which you did not cut the inner circle, remove the paper backing from a 1"-diameter circle and fuse it in the center of the shape.

4. Refer to the assembly diagram on page 63 to place the gears on the quilt top, or place them as desired. Fuse the gears *that do not cross seam lines* into place. You will need to remove the blocks from the design wall to do this. The remaining gears will be fused in place after the quilt top is assembled.

5. Stitch around the edges of the fused gears with a zigzag stitch. You can use a variegated, heavier thread and a wider zigzag stitch around the outside edges of the gears to resemble a serrated edge. You could also stitch baby rickrack to the outside edges to achieve this same effect. Stitch around the inner circle or hole with a narrower zigzag stitch. Return the blocks to your design wall as you finish them.

ASSEMBLING THE QUILT TOP

1. Sew the blocks in each row together. Press the seam allowances in opposite directions from row to row.

2. Sew the rows together. Press the seam allowances toward the bottom of the quilt top.

3. Fuse the remaining gears to the quilt top and stitch them in place. Your quilt top is done! Congratulations!

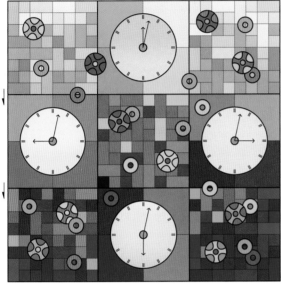

Quilt assembly

FINISHING THE QUILT

Referring to "Basic Quiltmaking Techniques," beginning on page 90, layer the quilt top with batting and backing fabric, and baste the layers together. Quilt as desired or choose a quilting design from "Quilting Ideas" on page 81. I added a little sparkle and sheen to this quilt by embellishing it with beads. For beading ideas and instructions, see "Embellishing Tools, Tips, and Techniques" on page 21. Bind the quilt with the 2"-wide binding strips.

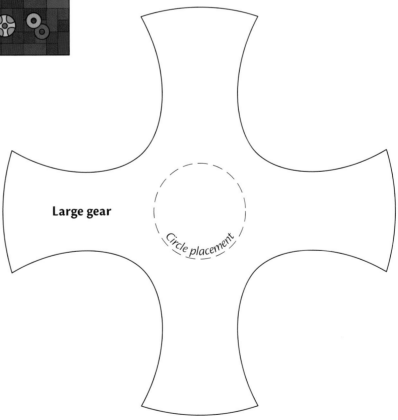

Large gear

Circle placement

PATRIOTIC BREEZES

The movement created by the blocks in this quilt reminds me of a Fourth of July picnic, complete with carefree children blowing on toy pinwheels and the bright burst of spectacular fireworks.

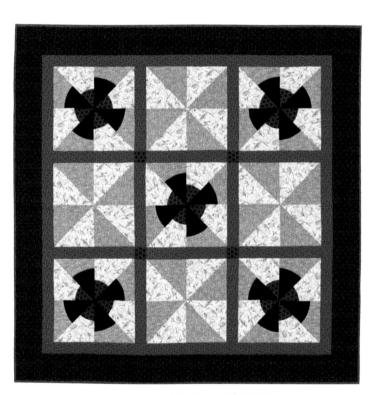

By Leigh E. McDonald, 2005

Skill Level: Beginner
Finished Quilt Size: 45" x 45"
Finished Block Size: 10½" x 10½"

MATERIALS

All yardages are based on 42"-wide fabric.

⅞ yard of white print for block backgrounds

⅞ yard of medium blue print for block backgrounds

⅞ yard of red print for sashing, inner border, and binding

⅔ yard of red-on-navy print for outer border

⅜ yard of navy print for blocks

¼ yard of navy-on-red print for blocks

3⅛ yards of fabric for backing (pieced crosswise)

51" x 51" piece of batting

CUTTING

All measurements include ¼"-wide seam allowances. Cut all strips across the width of the fabric.

From the white print, cut:
5 squares, 12½" x 12½"

From the medium blue print, cut:
5 squares, 12½" x 12½"

From the navy-on-red print, cut:
4 squares, 2" x 2"

From the red print, cut:
13 strips, 2" wide; crosscut 4 strips into 12 segments, 11" long

From the red-on-navy print, cut:
5 strips, 4" wide

MAKING THE BLOCKS

1. Refer to "Working with Circles" on page 16 to determine your preferred appliqué method. *For fusible appliqué*, use a yardstick compass set at 4⅝" to make three 9¼"-diameter circles from the navy print. Use the compass or circle cutter set at 3⅛" to make three 6¼"-diameter circles from the remaining navy-on-red print fabric. *For freezer-paper appliqué*, use the same compass/circle cutter settings as for fusible appliqué to make three 9¼"-diameter circle templates from freezer paper and three 6¼"-diameter circle templates from freezer paper. Press the 9¼"-diameter templates onto the navy fabric and the 6¼"-diameter templates onto the remaining navy-on-red print, and then use a rotary cutter, scissors, or circle cutter to cut out the fabric circles ⅜" larger than the freezer-paper circles.

2. Using the appliqué method you selected in step 1, appliqué a navy circle to three medium-blue squares, centering the circles in the squares. Repeat to appliqué a navy-on-red circle to three white print squares.

Make 3.

Make 3.

3. Place one of the navy-on-red print appliquéd squares in the corner of your cutting mat so that the lower-left corner of the square is at the 0 mark,

right side up. The bottom and left sides of the square should be aligned with the horizontal and vertical lines along the edges of the mat. Stack one of the navy print appliquéd squares on top of it, right side down, aligning the edges of the blocks.

4. Using your rotary cutter and long ruler to cut through the stacked squares, make a horizontal cut at the 6¼" line on the mat. Make a vertical cut at the 6¼" line. Carefully cut diagonally from corner to corner in both directions. You have divided the blocks into eight equal segments. Do not separate the layers; the pieces are in pairs and ready to sew!

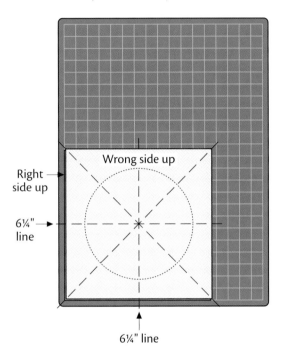

5. Pick up one pair of triangles and sew them together along the longest edges. The edges to be sewn have been cut along the bias, so be careful not to stretch them as you sew. Press the seam allowances toward the medium blue segments. Repeat with the remaining pairs. Each stacked pair of squares will yield four A units and four B units.

Unit A   Unit B

Speedy Sewing

To speed up the sewing of the units, chain piece all the triangle pairs from the layered squares, and then press them. You will be done in no time at all!

6. Sew the four A units together as shown to make block A, being careful to match points and outside edges. Press the seam allowances as indicated. Repeat with the four B units to make block B.

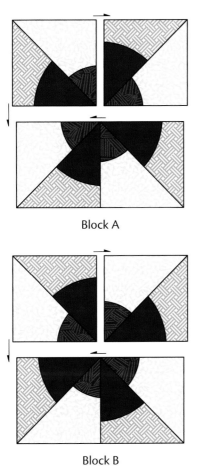

Block A

Block B

7. Repeat steps 3–6 with the remaining appliquéd squares to make three *each* of blocks A and B.

8. Refer to "Basic Quiltmaking Techniques" on page 90 to square up the blocks to 11" x 11". Make sure your ruler is centered on the block with the center point of the pinwheel at the 5½" mark on the ruler in both the horizontal and vertical directions. Pick the five best blocks to use in the wall hanging; set aside the leftover block for a future project.

9. Repeat steps 3–6 to stack one of the remaining white print 12½" squares and one of the remaining medium blue print 12½" squares together, and cut the layered pair into eight equal sections. Sew the pairs of triangles together along the longest edges to make half-square-triangle units. Press the seam allowances toward the medium-blue print. Repeat with the remaining white and medium blue squares to make a total of 16 units. Sew four units together to make a Pinwheel block. Make four. Square up the blocks to 11" x 11".

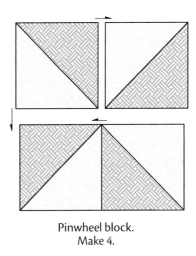

Pinwheel block.
Make 4.

ASSEMBLING THE QUILT TOP

1. Refer to the quilt assembly diagram on page 68 to arrange the blocks into three horizontal rows of three blocks each, inserting a red print 2" x 11" sashing segment between the blocks in each row.

2. Sew the blocks and sashing strips in each row together. Press the seam allowances toward the sashing strips.

3. To make the sashing rows, alternately sew three sashing strips and two navy-on-red print 2" squares together. Press the seam allowances toward the sashing strips.

4. With seams matching, sew the block rows and sashing rows together, inserting a sashing row between block rows. Press the seam allowances toward the sashing rows.

5. Carefully square up the quilt top. Use a square ruler for the corners and a long ruler and rotary cutter for the sides.

ADDING THE BORDERS

For general instructions on measuring and sewing borders, refer to "Adding Borders" on page 91.

1. Measure the quilt top for the inner side borders. Trim two of the remaining red print strips to the length measured, and sew them to the sides of the quilt top. Press the seam allowances toward the border strips.

2. Measure the quilt top for the inner top and bottom borders. Trim two of the remaining red print strips to the length measured, and sew them to the top and bottom of the quilt top. Press the seam allowances toward the border strips.

3. Measure the quilt top for the outer side borders. Trim two red-on-navy outer-border strips to the length measured, and sew the strips to the sides of the quilt. Press the seam allowances toward the outer-border strips.

4. Cut one of the remaining red-on-navy strips in half crosswise. Sew one half to each of the remaining red-on-navy strips. Measure the quilt for the top and bottom borders. Trim the pieced strips to the length measured, and sew the strips to the top and bottom of the quilt. Press the seam allowances toward the outer-border strips. Your top is finished!

FINISHING THE QUILT

Referring to "Basic Quiltmaking Techniques," beginning on page 90, layer the quilt top with batting and backing fabric, and baste the layers together. Quilt as desired. This quilt is perfect for stitching in the ditch. You could quilt along each sashing seam and along each seam of the blocks. See "Quilting Ideas" on page 81 for more quilting designs and suggestions. Bind the edges with the remaining red print 2"-wide strips.

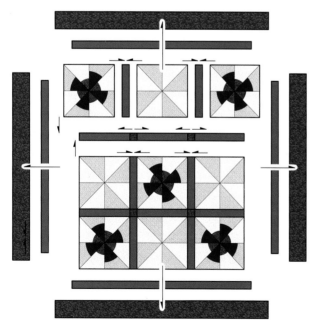

Quilt assembly

GALLERY

Some of the quilts here are variations of the project quilts, but others are expressions of my own imagination as well as that of other artists. Many thanks go to the artists who allowed me to include their work. I hope these quilts spur your imagination, excite your creativity, and inspire more ideas for ways to use circles in quilts. Enjoy the eye candy!

CIRCLE FOUR PATCH

By Leigh E. McDonald, 2005, 35½" x 35½". Batiks give this quilt a completely different feel than the larger version of the same design, "Nellie's Circle Four Patch" (page 31).

FOWL FANTASY III

By Susan Leslie Lumsden, 2005, 27" x 40". Inspired by a bouquet of feathers from a friend's chicken yard, Susan hand dyed silk fabrics and threw in a few metallics to re-create the arrangement. Feather quilting adds to the fowl theme. This quilt was influenced by the quilt "21st-Century Bull's Eye" in the book *Quilts from Aunt Amy* by Country Threads (Martingale & Company, 1999).

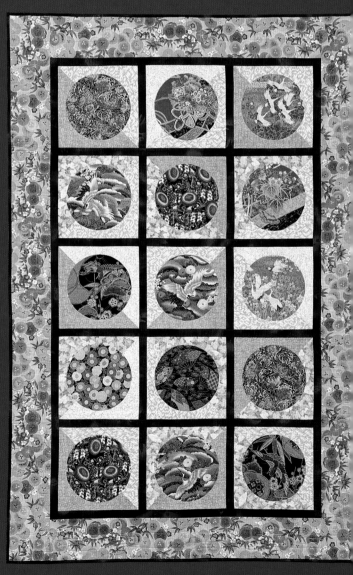

CIRCLES OF THE ORIENT

By Leigh E. McDonald, 2001, 44½" x 66". I was able to showcase my extensive collection of Asian-inspired fabrics in this quilt. The border is quilted with a bamboo design.

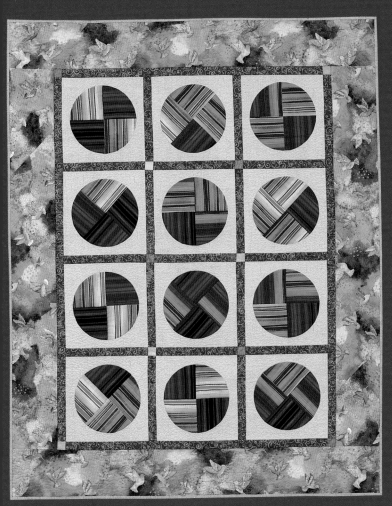

MONKEY'S FIST II

By Leigh E. McDonald, 2005,
45½" x 56½". Although the corner-stones in
the outer border have been eliminated, this
fanciful variation of the original "Monkey's
Fist" (page 35) is the same design.

EASY AS PIE

By Leigh E. McDonald, 2006,
54" x 64½". This quilt, a variation
of "Patriotic Breezes" (page 65)
and "Summer Breezes" at left, has
a plain setting square between
each pieced block, allowing an
opportunity to showcase the
quilting design. The quilting
design is a variation of the rose
border motif shown on page 89.

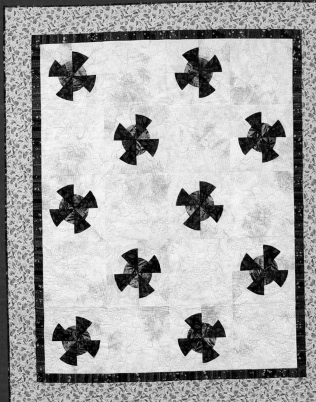

SUMMER BREEZES

By Leigh E. McDonald, 2005, 45" x 45".
This quilt is a variation of "Patriotic Breezes".
The secondary pinwheel design is highlighted
with blue green tulle.

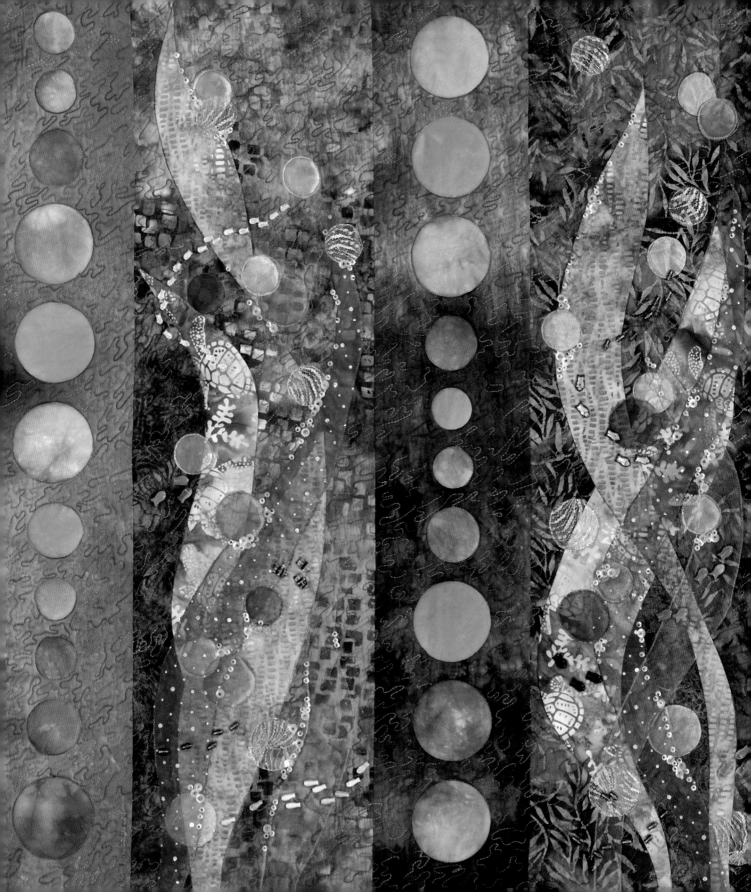

SEA WEEDS

By Leigh E. McDonald, 2006, 49½" x 32". This wall quilt is made from a mixture of hand-dyed sateen and batik fabrics. The bubbles are appliquéd and the seaweed is pieced. I had great fun collecting the different types of fish beads from shops all around the country. I used tulle and netting with holographic sequins for some of the seaweed shapes, and organza and a metallic lace for the bubbles.

MARBELOUS MARBLES

By Leigh E. McDonald, 2001, 26" x 33¼". My hand-dyed and painted fabrics were used to create this quilt, which uses a variation of the Drunkard's Path block. Quilting with metallic thread added a bit of sparkle to the background and borders.

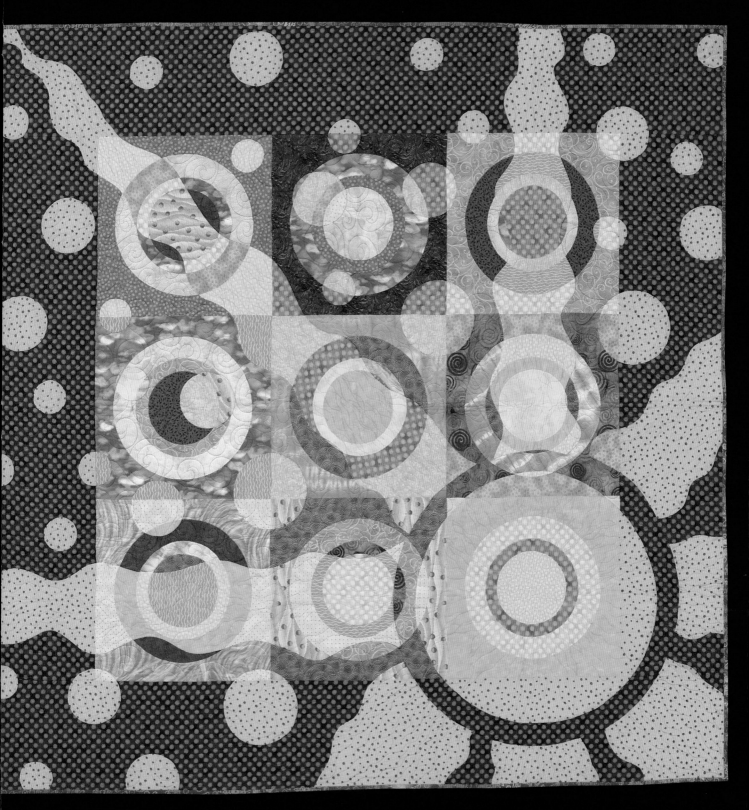

SUN SPOTS

By Kimberly Montagnese, 2004, 69" x 69". Kim used the sun appliqué as a way to break up the base design. Only after she finished the quilt did she notice that all the fabrics had a circular print of some kind.

GLASS BUBBLES

By Leigh E. McDonald, 2002,
44" x 36". I saved the little slivers
of fabric that were left after
squaring up the blocks from
"Marbelous Marbles" and used
them, along with the portions
of fabric I cut away from behind
the appliquéd circles of that
project, to make the sticks and
balls in this quilt.

REALLY, REALLY BROKEN DISHES

By Kimberly Montagnese, 2000, 60" x 83". This quilt was inspired by a broken piece of Kim's wedding china. The silver cording was couched on the blocks to resemble the cracks in the dish. The corner triangles were added to remind Kim of the search for all the broken chips.

CATCH A FALLING MOON

By Kim Svoboda, 2006, 52½" x 52½". Kim challenged herself to use a group of wonderful but very dissimilar batik circles and came up with this design. The hand-quilted waves flow with the circles.

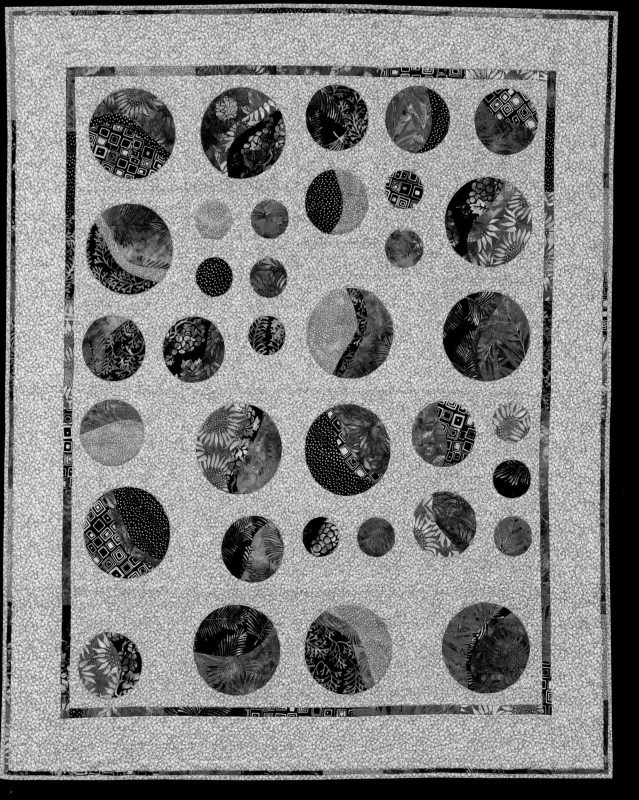

BATIK CIRCLES

By Leigh E. McDonald, 2005, 48½" x 59¾". Warm-colored batik fabrics and the addition of borders create a different feel for this variation of "Balls in the Air" (page 43). It is heavily quilted with a combination of the spiral and leaf motifs that can be found in "Quilting Ideas," beginning on page 81.

QUILTING IDEAS

Quilting gives a quilt top life. It adds dimension by sculpting the surface of the quilt. Without quilting, a top is unfinished and unusable. In this section, I have included information on classic quilting methods, as well as some ideas and actual patterns for more fanciful designs. These continuous-line designs are for machine quilters, but some of them can be adjusted to hand quilting by leaving out the carrying stitches that connect the motifs. Many of the designs given are filler patterns to use in the backgrounds around the appliquéd circles or in the borders.

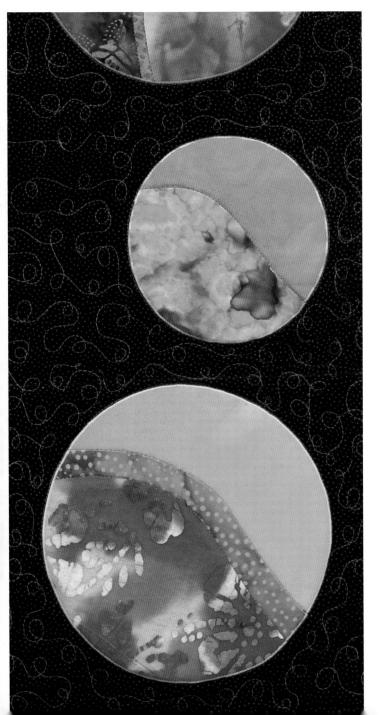

CLASSIC QUILTING METHODS

Quilting in the ditch, outline quilting, and echo quilting are classic methods for quilting your project that do not require marking your top.

Several of the quilts in this book have sashing and narrow borders. Quilting in the ditch next to these straight lines is an easy and effective way to quilt these areas. To quilt in the ditch, use your even-feed or walking foot and stitch next to the sashing or border strip. The stitches should fall on the side without the seam allowance. Use a thread color that matches the sashing or border in case you accidentally hop out of the ditch and onto these areas.

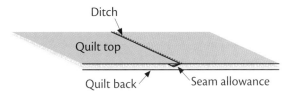

Outline quilting is another commonly used quilting method. For these quilts, stitch on the background fabric next to, not on, the appliquéd circles, following the shape of the appliqué. If you outline quilt around the circles and then fill in the remainder of the background with stippling or another filler pattern, the circles will be puffier and

"Balls in the Air" is quilted with the classic loop pattern.

pop out. Dense quilting flattens and compresses the batting while less quilting produces a puffier appearance. I used my even-feed or walking foot to stitch around the circles on most of the quilts, but smaller circles are often easier to quilt around using free-motion quilting, with the feed dogs down and a darning or free-motion quilting foot attached.

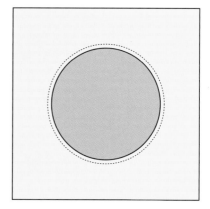

Outline quilting

You can also echo quilt the background of the block by stitching around the circle and then repeating the shape with concentric lines of quilting until the background is filled. Use the edge of your presser foot as a guide and fill in the background only. On some quilts this makes a secondary design of a curved diamond where the lines of stitching come together. I used this technique on "Circles in the Attic" on page 39.

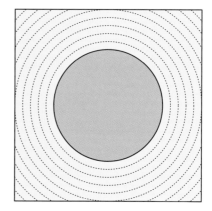

Echo quilting

"Monkey's Fist" uses the loops-and-butterflies quilting pattern.

FANCIFUL QUILTING DESIGNS

To use the quilting designs, start by tracing one of the designs that begins on page 84 onto tracing paper or deli paper. Make a test quilt sandwich, using a couple of the fabrics in your quilt on top of a layer of the batting and backing you plan to use. This way you can test out the design, the threads, the batting, and the backing to make sure everything is compatible. It is no fun to start quilting on the actual piece and have your thread break every 4" or discover that the quilting design is overpowering your fabrics. Testing allows you time to practice and reduces the pressure to be perfect the first time you quilt the design. On a test piece, who cares if it's not perfect!

Place the paper with the traced quilt design on top of your test quilt sandwich and pin it in place. With the feed dogs down or disabled and the darning foot or free-motion quilting foot attached, stitch, following the pattern lines through the paper and quilt sandwich. Remove pins as you stitch. Tear away the paper when you are done stitching. When you have practiced enough to get the rhythm of the quilt design, try it without the tracing paper. I do not recommend doing a whole quilt using the paper pattern; it is too much work to tear all that paper away when you are done stitching. Plus, I think it is more interesting to see the variation that happens in each quilter's stitched designs when they are "drawing" it without the aid of a traced pattern.

Many of these designs are great for filling in a background. These designs do not have to be perfect; each quilter develops a personal style when stitching a filler design. Some quilters stitch rounded circles, some more elongated. Some leaves have pointed edges, some are rounded. Your stipples may look slightly different from mine, but it does not mean they are wrong! If you are insecure about your quilting, practice lots *and* use a thread color that matches the fabric. This will hide any bobbles you might make.

"Easy as Pie" is quilted with a variation of the rose border pattern.

Stipple and loop designs are tried and true. They have multiple uses and endless variations. Enlarge them for borders or reduce them for heavy background quilting. These patterns are often the basis for other filler patterns.

Spirals and stipples combine to make a good background quilting pattern. The spiral and stipple pattern takes practice to perfect because the spirals have a rhythm and direction to them that differs from the stipple design. Spiral suns enclose the spirals with a wavy line and a large zigzagging line alternately. This pattern was used to quilt "Clockworks" on page 59.

Combining a butterfly motif with the loop pattern makes a fun quilting design for a child's quilt. I used this pattern for "Monkey's Fist" on page

35. The quilting design reinforced the theme of the quilt with its printed butterflies in the border fabric.

The rose spiral pattern is an allover, continuous-line filler pattern. This would be a great pattern to choose when you have a lot of background to quilt, because the pattern is larger. The rose border would be a good design to use in a border. You can customize the pattern to fit your border by making it narrower or wider.

Use your imagination to create new designs for your quilting projects. By combining designs you can come up with some I haven't discovered yet. I hope the designs I have given here will excite your own creativity. Enjoy quilting your circle quilts!

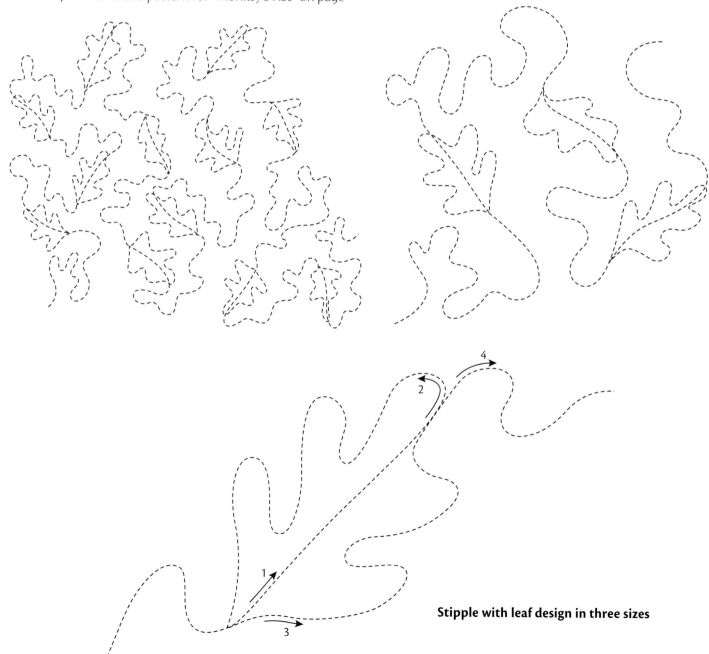

Stipple with leaf design in three sizes

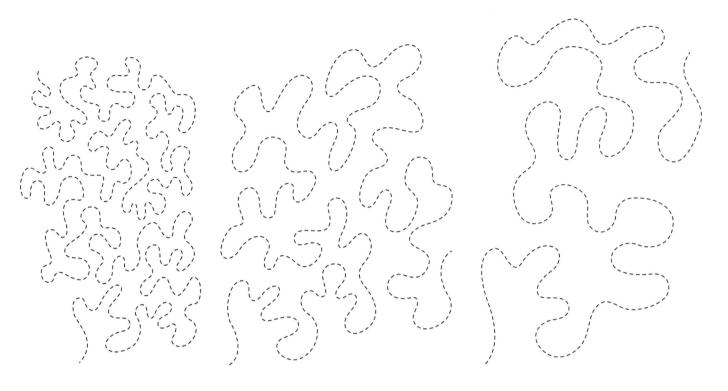

Classic stipple design in three sizes

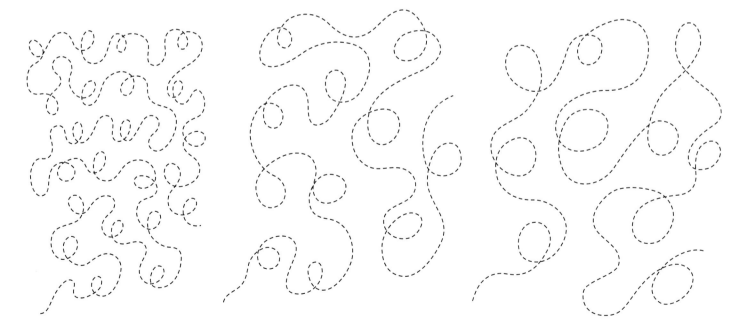

Classic loop design in three sizes

Spiral with leaf in two sizes

Spiral stipple in two sizes

Spiral suns

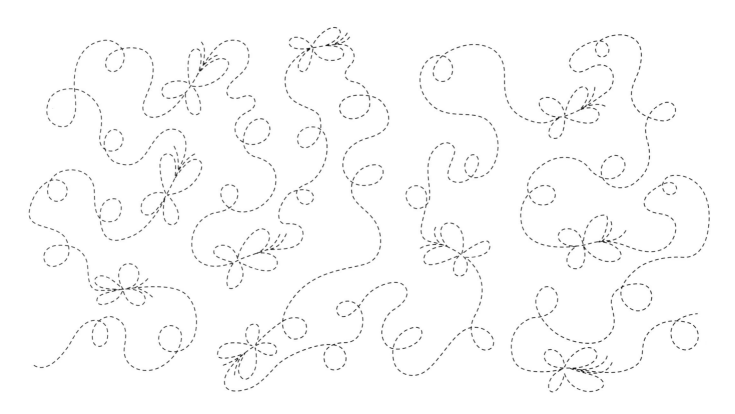

Loops and butterflies

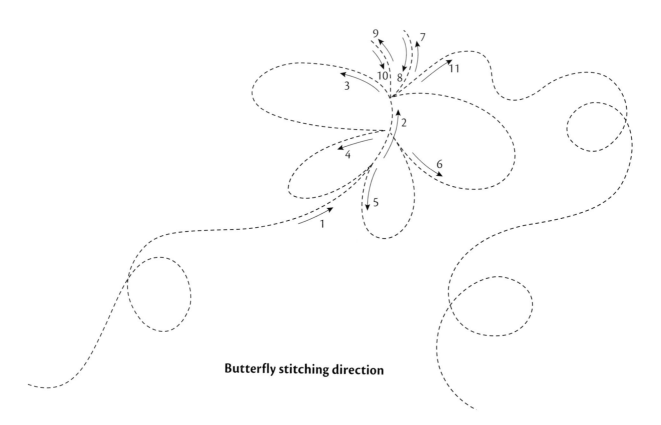

Butterfly stitching direction

Rose spirals

Rose border

BASIC QUILTMAKING TECHNIQUES

This section is not a comprehensive guide that includes every step involved in making a quilt. What it does include are techniques that I find are always good to review, as well as instructions for techniques that I refer to throughout the projects.

SEWING A MITERED SEAM

Mitered seams have a variety of uses, and sewing them is a good technique to know. I use mitered seams most commonly when sewing two border or binding strips together. It reduces the bulkiness or thickness in a binding and in a border it helps to hide the piecing line when dealing with prints where a straight piecing line would show.

To make a mitered seam, take two strips that are the same width and any length. Lay the ends of the strips right sides together at right angles as shown. Angle the strips under the sewing-machine needle and sew a diagonal line, beginning at the notch formed by the meeting of the two strips and sewing toward the notch at the lower edge. Use a short stitch length when sewing the strips together. Check your seam to make sure the two strips line up in a continuous strip. After checking the seam, cut the threads and trim the seam allowance to ¼". Press the seam allowance to one side.

SQUARING UP A BLOCK

Lots of things can happen when you're making your blocks that will result in corners that aren't perfectly square—inaccurate cutting, variations in pressing techniques, and inconsistencies in stitching can all cause this result. In order for your quilt to have square corners and hang straight, your blocks need to have square corners as well.

To square up a block, you will need a square ruler that is the same size as or larger than the *unfinished* block. Using the measurements on the ruler that correspond to the block's unfinished size, center the ruler on the block. Make sure that the center line of the square on the ruler is aligned with the block center. For example, if your unfinished block is 11½", then the 5¾" vertical and horizontal marks on the ruler should intersect at the block center. Be sure that the appliqué is also centered. Trim any excess along the top and right edges of the ruler. Rulers tend to slide when doing this so be careful not to move it. Rotate the block 180°. Center the ruler on the block again, with the block's newly trimmed edges aligned with the lines on the ruler that correspond with the unfinished block measurement. Trim the excess along the top and right edges.

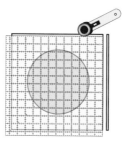 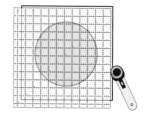

Trim 2 sides.　　　　Rotate block.
　　　　　　　　　Trim remaining 2 sides.

Centering the Ruler

When squaring up a block that has triangles, such as the blocks in "Patriotic Breezes" (page 65), line up a diagonal line on the ruler with the diagonal lines in the triangle block. You want to make sure the diagonal line in the triangle still goes through the corner of the block.

ADDING BORDERS

Once the center of your quilt is pieced, you are ready to add borders (if your quilt design calls for them). The project instructions will specify the width of the border strips and the number of strips to cut. To ensure that the borders fit your quilt, you'll need to follow the steps below to measure the quilt top and cut the borders to the exact size. By doing so, you will avoid problems with wavy edges on your quilts. I usually add the side borders first and then the top and bottom borders, but not always, so be sure to follow the project instructions.

1. For the side borders, measure the length of the quilt top along the outside left edge, the outside right edge, and through the center. I write down each of the measurements, noting which measurement is which. If the measurements do not all match but are within ¼" of each other, I average the three measurements. For instance, if your top measures 53¼" on the left edge, 53⅛" on the right edge, and 53" through the center, you are still within ¼" on all measurements. The average of the three measurements is 53⅛". If any of the measurements differ by more than ¼", you will need to adjust some of the seam allowances to reduce the discrepancy. Either take wider seam allowances on some of the seams to reduce the measurement or take narrower seam allowances to increase the measurement. The seams cannot vary by more than ¼" because you can't ease more than ¼" of excess without forming a pleat or having your seams start to come apart where you are attaching the border to the center. Of course the best scenario is when all your measurements are off by only ⅛" or so, but we don't live in a perfect world!

Write Down Your Measurements

If you know the measurements have to be within ¼" of each other, you will mentally adjust them in your mind so that they work. We can rationalize anything, especially if we don't really want to resew any seams! When you write them down it keeps you honest and in the long run will make the process easier when you sew on the borders.

2. After you have your final measurement for the side borders, cut the border strips to the correct length. You may need to sew strips together to create strips that are long enough and then trim them to the exact length. Sew your strips together using a mitered seam. Fold the strips in half and then in half again. Mark the folds with pins. This divides your border length into quarters. Do the same with the side edges of the quilt top. Fold the edges in half and then in half again and mark the folds with pins. Pin the borders to the quilt top, matching pin marks, and then go back and add pins about every 5".

3. With the border strip on the top and the quilt top on the bottom, sew the borders to the top. This helps ease in any excess you may have in the quilt center. Press the seam allowances toward the borders, unless the quilt project instructs otherwise.

4. Measure the width of the quilt top in the same manner, including the side borders in the measurements. Cut the strips to the exact length, piecing if necessary, and then sew them to the quilt top in the same manner as the side borders. Press the seam allowances toward the borders, unless otherwise instructed.

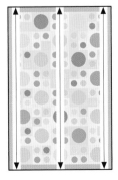

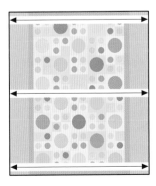

LAYERING A QUILT

Before you can quilt your project, you must layer the top, batting, and backing together to make a quilt sandwich. The backing and batting should be anywhere from 4" to 8" bigger than your quilt top. The larger the project, the more I add. This means that your backing may need to be pieced to be large enough. None of the projects in this book require more than two lengths to achieve the backing size needed. The yardage for each project will indicate if the seam needs to run lengthwise or crosswise to make use of the amount of fabric given. Remove the selvages before sewing the lengths together and press the seam allowance to one side.

To assemble the quilt sandwich:

1. Place the pressed backing fabric *right side down* on a table or tile floor that is larger than the quilt. Use masking tape to secure the backing to the surface so that it remains flat throughout the remaining steps.

2. Fold your batting in half and then in half again. Place the batting in one corner of the quilt backing with the center fold in the center of the backing fabric. Make sure to lift the batting when you move it; do not let it drag on the backing fabric or it will move the backing fabric and you will get wrinkles or tucks when you go to quilt. Carefully unfold the batting over the backing and smooth it out, working from the center to the outside edges. Keep checking the backing fabric to make sure there are no wrinkles.

3. Fold the quilt top into quarters and place it on the batting in the same manner that you placed the batting on the backing. You should have a few extra inches of batting and backing on all sides of the quilt sandwich. Make sure the edges of the quilt top are parallel to the edges of the backing fabric. Gently smooth the quilt top over the batting. If you are using cotton batting, pick up the edge of the quilt top to allow air between the top and the batting, and then smooth the top onto the batting with your other hand, working from the center to the outside edges. Cotton batting clings to the fabric and if you try to smooth the quilt top without lifting it first, you'll just add creases.

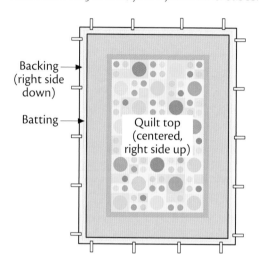

Backing (right side down)

Batting

Quilt top (centered, right side up)

4. Once you have layered your quilt sandwich, you are ready to baste the quilt layers together so they don't shift when you are quilting. I machine quilt and my favorite method of basting is to pin baste.

Preparing Your Quilt Top

Before you layer your quilt, there is a little housekeeping you need to do to make the quilt top ready for quilting. Turn your quilt top over so that you can see all the seams. Check the seams to make sure there are no twists in the seam allowances. If a seam allowance is twisted, it will often leave a bulge when you quilt, so you want to fix this now. Just clip a couple of threads at the seam allowance, press the seam back in the direction of the rest of the seam, and stitch the seam allowance once more to secure the seam. Most of the time there are only a few of these seams to fix. You also want to cut all thread tails and any frayed edges that might show through to the front. That means dark threads on light fabric. If you don't deal with these now they will show up once you have quilted the piece and there's no way to correct them then.

The pins are easy to remove when quilting and when you are done, there are no basting threads to take out. To pin baste, insert 1"-long quilter's safety pins about 4" apart over the entire quilt top. I use the width of my hand as a guide for the distance between the pins. Start at the center and work across the width of the quilt to the outer edges, then work vertically. This divides the quilt into four quarters. Fill in the quarters with pins. Avoid placing pins at any seam lines you plan to quilt. Plan ahead so that, if possible, you can quilt without having to remove a safety pin.

Closing Safety Pins

Place all your pins in the quilt sandwich before closing the pins. This keeps the quilt sandwich from moving when you close the pins. A great tool for this job is the Kwik Klip. It enables you to quickly close the safety pins without reaching under the quilt with your other hand or ruining your fingernails trying to close all those safety pins.

ATTACHING A HANGING SLEEVE

Many of the quilts in the book are wall-hanging size. If you want to hang your quilt, add a hanging sleeve after you quilt the quilt and before you bind it.

1. Trim the backing and batting ⅛" larger than the top, using a square ruler in the corners and a long ruler on the edges.

2. For small wall hangings, cut a piece of backing fabric 9" wide by the width of your quilt top less 1". For large wall hangings such as "Clockworks," cut a piece of backing fabric 9" wide by the width of the quilt top less 2". Then cut the piece in half crosswise to make two equal pieces. You will leave 1" of space in the center of the backing between the two pieces. This distributes the weight of the quilt better and allows you to add support at the center of the wall hanging as well as at the outer edges.

3. Finish the short edges of your casing(s) by folding them under ¼" twice and sewing them down with a straight stitch next to the folded edge. Fold the casing in half lengthwise and pin the raw edges

to the top edge of the quilt top. Remember to leave 1" of space between the two casings for large wall hangings. Using a longer stitch length, machine baste the casing in place just inside the seam allowance along the top edge.

4. Pin the fold to the quilt to keep it in place and out of the way when adding the binding. Bind the quilt, following the instructions below. The raw edges of the sleeve will be enclosed in the binding.

5. To keep your quilt lying flat when it is hanging on a rod or slat, allow excess in the casing fold. To do this I move the outside folded edge up just a little to allow some slack for the rod to sit. Then I sew the folded edge to the back of the quilt using a tiny appliqué stitch and keeping the distance between stitches less than ¼". Sometimes the casing will wear at the bottom folded edge and pull away from the quilt top. To reinforce the stitching, I start stitching the folded edge 1" into the casing and work my way toward the outside finished edge, sewing away from the center of the quilt top. I put two stitches in the corner and then stitch over my stitches going back toward the center of the quilt. I do this on the other end also. This just reinforces the stitching so it will not break or wear as easily.

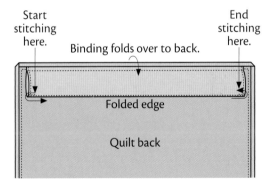

BINDING THE QUILT EDGES

I like to bind my quilts with a French, or double-fold, binding. All the projects give fabric amounts for this type of binding, and all the strips are cut across the width of the fabric. Before you begin, you will need to piece the strips together using a mitered seam (refer to "Sewing a Mitered Seam" on page 90) to make one continuous binding strip.

1. Cut the beginning of the binding strip at a 45° angle and press the raw edge to the wrong side

½". Fold the binding strip in half lengthwise, wrong sides together, and press the fold.

2. Starting at one of the side edges below the center point, place the binding on the top of the quilt, aligning the raw edges. Using a ¼" seam allowance, stitch the binding to the quilt top through all the layers, starting 6" from the beginning of the binding; backstitch. Continue sewing until you are ¼" from the first corner; backstitch. Remove the quilt from the machine.

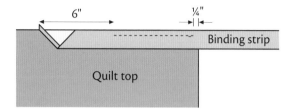

3. Fold the binding strip up so the fold forms a 45° angle. Maintaining the angled fold, fold the binding back down to create a second fold that is even with the raw edges at the corner. Pin the corner in place. Begin stitching at the fold, backstitch, and then stitch to within ¼" of the next corner. Repeat the folding and stitching at each corner.

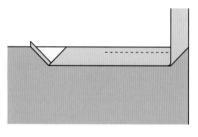

4. When you are 6" from the beginning of the strip, backstitch and remove the quilt from the machine. Lay the end of the binding strip over the beginning and trim it so there is a 1" overlap. Tuck the end of the strip inside the beginning of the strip. Continue to sew the binding in place.

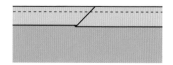

5. Fold the binding to the back of the quilt top and stitch it in place with tiny appliqué stitches, mitering and stitching the corners in the same direction as on the front of the quilt. Also stitch the folded edge at the beginning of the binding. Try to make your stitches invisible.

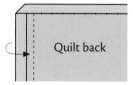 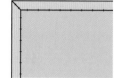

Machine-Stitched Binding

If you want to add a binding totally by machine, pin the binding to the *back* of the quilt top and stitch it in place according to the instructions above. Fold the binding to the front and stitch it in place by machine. For a hand-stitched look, use a blind hem stitch and monofilament thread. Otherwise, use a straight stitch. The corners and beginning edge will still need to be stitched by hand.

BURYING THREAD ENDS

Even though I machine quilt my quilts, I feel it is important to hide the thread ends rather than just cutting them off even with the quilt top. Burying the threads makes the quilt stronger and the quilting stitches are less likely to come out. To bury threads, I use an embroidery needle with a large eye and a sharp point. I give the threads a tug and then feed two of them at a time through the needle. With the tip of the needle I go into the top layer of the quilt at the point where the threads come out, and carry the needle tip between the top and the batting layer for approximately ¼" before coming back out of the quilt top. I pull the threads all the way through the layers and give them a good tug before cutting the threads even with the quilt-top fabric. The cut ends of the thread lie between the layers of the quilt and are no longer visible on the front.

RESOURCES

If you can't find the supplies you need at your local quilt shop, I recommend the resources listed below.

Artfabrik, Inc.
Laura Wasilowski
324 Vincent Place
Elgin, IL 60123
847-931-7684
www.artfabrik.com
Hand-dyed fabrics and threads.

Clotilde, LLC
PO Box 7500
Big Sandy, TX 75755-7500
800-772-2891
www.clotilde.com
Sewing notions, patterns, and books. Free catalog.

Fire Mountain Gems and Beads
One Fire Mountain Way
Grants Pass, OR 97526-2373
800-355-2137
www.firemountaingems.com
Beads and beading supplies. Free catalog.

Hancock's of Paducah
3841 Hinkleville Road
Paducah, KY 42001
800-845-8723
www.hancocks-paducah.com
Lots of fabrics. Free catalog.

Keepsake Quilting
Box 1618
Center Harbor, NH 03226
800-865-9458
www.keepsakequilting.com
Quilting fabrics, books, and supplies. Free catalog.

Meinke Toy
www.meinketoy.com
Online-only source for books on machine embroidery, hand beading, and a variety of innovative new products to add dimension and texture to your quilts.

Nancy's Notions
333 Beichl Ave.
PO Box 683
Beaver Dam, WI 53916-0683
800-833-0690
www.nancysnotions.com
Sewing notions, fabrics, patterns, and books. Free catalog.

Shipwreck Beads
8560 Commerce Drive NE
Lacey, WA 98516
800-950-4232
www.shipwreckbeads.com
Terrific source for beads of all kinds. Catalog available.

Superior Threads
87 E. 2580 South
St. George, UT 84790
800-499-1777
www.superiorthreads.com
Wonderful threads for quilting and embellishments, as well as a variety of educational tools and reference guides for threads.

Treenway Silks
501 Musgrave Road
Salt Spring Island, BC
Canada V8K 1V5
888-383-7455
www.treenwaysilks.com
Silk fibers, yarns and ribbons.

MEET THE AUTHOR

Photography by Paul Tople

Leigh E. McDonald has been sewing since childhood and quilting for 17 years. She teaches her contemporary quilting techniques internationally and her art quilts are in both private and public collections.

As a teenager Leigh moved around the country with her family, and the trend continued after she married her best friend and the love of her life in 1976. As a result of this nomadic existence, Leigh has a fascination for the differences among people, their speech, and their way of life. She enjoys drawing upon her passion for people and places while sharing her quilting expertise.

Her latest big adventure is a return to college to get a bachelor's degree in fine arts. Leigh is a new transplant to Covington, Kentucky, where she lives with her husband of 32 years near their two adult children.

For information about Leigh's art quilts, lectures, or workshops, visit her Web site at www.adventuresinquilting.com.